Leicester's Ghost

VOLUME IV OF THE PUBLICATIONS

OF THE RENAISSANCE ENGLISH TEXT SOCIETY

Thomas Rogers

Leicester's Ghost

EDITED BY FRANKLIN B. WILLIAMS, JR.

Published for

The Newberry Library

by

The University of Chicago Press

International Standard Book Number: 0-226-72372-0

Library of Congress Catalog Card Number: 74-159785

THE UNIVERSITY OF CHICAGO PRESS, CHICAGO 60637
The University of Chicago Press, Ltd., London

Contents

List of Illustrations / vi

Preface / vii

Introduction / ix
The legend of Robert Dudley / ix
Leicester's Ghost: *form, date, authorship* / xi
Thomas Rogers of Bryanston / xvi
The text: sources, editorial principles / xvii

Leicester's Ghost / 1

Notes / 87

Index of Persons / 91

Illustrations

Leicester's Bear Badge / xii

Woodcut from *La Vie abominable* / xiii

Preface

Since the Renaissance English Text Society publishes texts rather than literary history, the apparatus to this edition is limited to necessary background facts, statement of editorial principles, selected variant readings, minimal notes, and an identifying index of Tudor names. If the poem seems prejudiced against Leicester, the other side of the picture is easily found in Eleanor Rosenberg's splendid study, *Leicester: Patron of Letters* (1955).

It is impossible to acknowledge in detail the generosity of libraries and scholars who have helped the editor while and since he completed his 1934 Harvard dissertation on this text. The trustees of the British Museum and the trustees of the Newberry Library kindly permit the use of manuscripts as copytext, and the Bodleian Library and Christ Church, Oxford, have authorized the collation of the other manuscripts. Illustrations derive from the Folger Library and the British Museum. A travel grant from the American Council of Learned Societies during my sabbatical from Georgetown in 1967 enabled me to recheck the manuscripts and complete work at the Public Record Office.

FRANKLIN B. WILLIAMS, JR.

Introduction

THE LEGEND OF ROBERT DUDLEY

Robert Dudley, Earl of Leicester, was either the most libeled Elizabethan or one of the most callous villains in English history—perhaps both. The question need not be resolved in a study of literary fortunes rather than historical truth. During those very years when Leicester was achieving his deserved reputation as a patron of letters that has been analyzed by Eleanor Rosenberg, his political and religious enemies were assiduously collecting gossip. Perfected in a substantial book by Catholic exiles, the libels were published at Paris in the autumn of 1584 as *The Copie of a Leter, Wryten by a Master of Arte of Cambrige.* This book was smuggled into England but suppressed by royal proclamation on 12 October. Examples are accordingly rare, but the work proliferated amazingly in manuscript despite fresh official action in June 1585. Additional scandals were appended to a 1585 French version, *La Vie abominable de Lecestre Machiaueliste.* A Latin abridgment of the choicer matter was included by Julius Briegerus in *Flores Caluinistici*, twice printed at Milan in the same year. Referred to for a time as "Father Parsons' greencoat," *The Copie* soon acquired—from a marginal note (p. 52)—its permanent title of *Leicester's Commonwealth.*

The sensation created by *Leicester's Commonwealth* was largely due to the adroitness with which the case against the earl was presented. The skill in capturing interest, the air of patriotic impartiality, and the management of plausible detail rival or surpass Greene, Nashe, and Deloney. Despite the queen's indignation and the Privy Council's condemnation, despite formal refutation by nephew Sir Philip Sidney (holograph manuscript at the Morgan Library), despite a posthumous defense in the poetic anthology *The Phoenix Nest, Leicester's Commonwealth* was absorbed into the mind of the age. Libels from the *Commonwealth* and the later *Ghost* were perpetuated by generations of chroniclers such as Camden, John Clapham, Sir Robert Naunton, Gervase Holles, Francis Osborne, David Lloyd, and Elias Ashmole. On the stage they were echoed in *A Yorkshire Tragedy* (scene v) and in greater detail, as F. L. Lucas has shown, in *The White Devil*. They are reflected in a wry manuscript epitaph and in Ben Jonson's conversations with Drummond. Two elaborate versions were written in the decade 1595–1605. The first, an unprinted prose tract in the British Museum (MS. Sloane 1926), recounts Leicester's application at heaven's gate. The second is the elaborate verse paraphrase here edited. Interest revived with the lapse of press censorship in 1641. Despite official concern shown in the state papers (*CSPD 1641–1643*, p. 136), the *Commonwealth* was now twice reprinted, with the *Ghost* as an appendix; public demand was further attested by a prose epitome (Wing L969a). The next revival was a 1706 reprint disguised as *Secret Memoirs of Robert Dudley* "now published from an old manuscript" (two editions and two reissues down to 1721). The *Memoirs*, in turn, were a major source for Samuel Jebb's 1727 *Life*.

The approach of the romantic movement accounts for the fact that thenceforth interest concentrates on Leicester's first wife, Amy Robsart. Although Sir Walter Scott was chiefly responsible, the story begins with the 1784 imitation ballad "Cumnor Hall," written from Ashmole by James Mickle. More curiously, Scott was anticipated by John Keats. A letter of 17 November 1819 shows Keats planning a tragedy on Leicester; nothing survives unless one credits Sidney Colvin's pleasant vagary that the eerie fragment "This living hand" was written as a speech for Amy. Scott's free invention *Kenilworth* was a smash hit in 1821, and the worldwide spread of the story begins then. That Scott used the *Commonwealth* is easily demonstrable; that he used the *Ghost* eludes proof. The impact of *Kenilworth* is clear from six dramatic versions staged in the year of publication, followed by other plays and ballets. The story interested France in 1821 as in 1585, prompting Victor Hugo's early play *Amy*

Introduction

Robsart. Over the past century imaginative reconstructions—before and after Sabatini—have shared attention with efforts to establish the historical facts. The bibliography is lengthy. Even illiterate Elizabethans would understand the constant references to bears in the *Commonwealth* and the *Ghost*, for they knew that the great households of the Dudleys wore liveries with the crest of the white bear chained to the ragged staff. In concocting an imposing pedigree, the Dudleys preempted armorial devices from many sources; their favorite was the bear badge of the Beauchamps, assumed when John Dudley became earl of Warwick. This bear is the most striking feature of the handsome Dudley tombs in the Beauchamp Chapel of Saint Mary's, Warwick. The bear is at its most charming in the cub crouched at the feet of that "noble impe" of the Dudley blood, Leicester's lamented son Lord Denbigh. Elsewhere in Warwick it is displayed at Leicester's Hospital, together with the Sidney porcupine of the next holder of the earldom. Properly dignified with the garter, the crest was gold-stamped on the bindings in Leicester's library and is often reproduced in books dedicated to him (i.e., *STC* 4461, 5952, 11190, 22229, 24777, 25438). It was mentioned by poets, as by Geoffrey Whitney in *A Choice of Emblemes:* "Two Beares there are, the greater, and the lesse" —for though he was elder brother, good-natured Ambrose was content to be Ursa Minor. The most curious representation is the emblematic woodcut prefixed to *La Vie abominable*, a chained bear baited by dogs and other beasts. A natural suspicion that this woodcut was borrowed from an earlier non-Leicester book cannot be confirmed; Ruth Mortimer, the authority on French illustration of the period, suggests privately that it was probably commissioned for *La Vie*.

LEICESTER'S GHOST: *FORM, DATE, AUTHORSHIP*

Mainly a paraphrase of the *Commonwealth* in content, in form *Leicester's Ghost* is a rhyme royal "tragedy" in the tradition of *A Mirror for Magistrates*. The genre was enjoy-

LEICESTER'S BEAR BADGE
Geoffrey Whitney, *Emblemes*, 1586, sig. O1ʳ. Folger Library

AV LECTEVR SVR
cette image.

Et Ours (Amy lecteur) que tu vois tant syl-
   uestre,
Outrageux & felon, rempli de Cruauté,
C'est le Comte inhumain, le Comte de Leceftre,
Qui surpasse les Ours par sa ferocité.

THE BEAR BAITED
La Vie abominable, 1585. British Museum

ing its final vogue from 1599 to 1615, cultivated alike by poetasters and poets. Apart from the fat *Mirror* supplement by Richard Niccols, tragedies of Oldcastle, Lady Elizabeth Gray, Richard III, Wolsey, and Cromwell were published.

The assumption in older books that *Leicester's Ghost* is a Caroline anachronism rests on ignorance that the 1641 editions are not merely abridged but are modernized at lines 14 and 579. Details in the original text, such as the welcome to newly crowned James I, make it clear that the poem was completed not later than 1605. For instance, the praise of Sir Robert Dudley (line 2178) would not have been written after general knowledge of his romantic flight in July 1605, and the treatment of young Essex (line 678) reflects the opening of the reign. A *terminus a quo* is the 1601 execution of Essex the father (line 677), for the marginal notice of the 1603 death of Hunsdon (line 296n) may have been an addition. That parts may have been completed before the death of Elizabeth can be inferred from the fact that stanzas 155–68 on the succession became obsolete under James (apart from the awkward survival of Lady Arbella); they were properly deleted when the poem was abridged. To sum up, although parts may have been drafted earlier, it is safe to assign the long text to 1602–4.

The problem of authorship is solved by the unique manuscript of the original version, long unnoticed in the British Museum. This manuscript not merely identifies the writer as a Thomas Rogers, Esq., but certifies that it was his personal copy. Literary parallels that need not be rehearsed, confirmed by family connections, indicate that this particular possessor of a common name was the minor poet Thomas Rogers of Bryanston whose life is sketched in the next section. In particular, his connection with the countess of Hertford, for whom he wrote the memorial *Elegies*, explains his share in the Howard enmity toward Leicester, for the countess was sister to that Lady Sheffield whom Leicester had cast off. Similarly the *Commonwealth*'s concern with the royal succession fascinated Rogers for the good reason that his half-sister Honora was married to one of the pretenders, Lord Beauchamp of the Seymours. Doubtless the poet read Father Parsons' notorious *Conference about the Next Succession*, 1594, which would inform him that Beauchamp's match weakened his good chances, since, though of Puritan sympathies (p. 243), the Rogers family was of small consequence (p. 250). On his mother's side too the poet inherited a lively interest in public affairs. Indeed, in his mother's descent from the Lords De la Warr, the poet had a great-grandfather in common with Leicester himself.

With this interest in matters of state, Thomas Rogers paraphrased wholesale from the *Commonwealth*. A curious blunder (see note to line 544) indicates that he worked from one of the numerous manuscripts rather than a printed copy. Oral tradition supplied a few details (note to line 606). For the events of the earl's last four years he had to search elsewhere. Since he was only ten in 1584, he must have had other help than his memory, but no specific sources have been detected for his account of the Netherlands campaign, the Armada, and the earl's death. The treatment parallels Camden's *Annals*, and except for the awkward fact that Rogers wrote before the *Annals* were printed, one would argue that stanza 231 paraphrases Camden's opening lines on the year 1588.

After completing the *Ghost*, Rogers lived only a few years in ill health. There is no evidence that he attempted to print his dangerous poem, and the extent of manuscript circulation is uncertain. It is an open question whether Rogers wrote the marginal notes extant in two manuscripts. The seven stray marginalia in his own manuscript fit in with but do not prove that he compiled the extensive set in the Phillipps manuscript, though a few of these contain information not in the text (e.g., lines 141n, 205n, 211n). It is even more doubtful whether he managed the abridgment found in most surviving texts. Cutting the length by more than a third was a good idea; one gladly spares long political preachments and the dreary review of the succession. On the other hand, it is hard to believe that the author would have sacrificed interesting stanzas on Tilbury Camp and the earl's death, material never printed until now.

Rhyme royal tragedies are a Drab Age genre. Rogers of Bryanston had a facile but uninspired command of the conventions: metrical regularity, frequent moralizing, poetical commonplaces and rhetorical devices, stock classical allusions, and appeals to English history. There are no passages to anthologize. As the notes point out, the *Ghost* echoes previous books—not merely the poet's own sonnets, but works by Castiglione, Kyd, Spenser, Drayton, and Anon. Whether the poet's or an editor's, the notion of abridging was sound in concept, faulty in execution.

THOMAS ROGERS OF BRYANSTON

Thomas Rogers (1574–1609?) was the son of Sir Richard Rogers of Bryanston, a Dorset squire of the Armada years, by his second wife, Mary West of the noble De la Warr family. Through marriages of his half-sisters on both sides, he was linked with the noble Seymour family and with Sir George More of Loseley, Donne's father-in-law. He matriculated at Oxford in 1584, was graduated A.B. in 1590, proceeded to New Inn, and entered the Middle Temple in 1591. Spoiled and thriftless, he frequented London society and sank into debts that kept him many months in the Poultry Counter. He was victim of the droll incident that, as the late C. J. Sisson discovered, provided Ben Jonson with his gull Dapper in *The Alchemist*. During the ill health of his later years he lived in London, Normandy, and Oxford, but mostly at Bryanston. After his father's death in 1605, much of his time was spent in law suits over his heritage. These were still in progress when he died in December 1609 or January 1610. Meanwhile, to his family's chagrin, he had dabbled in verse. The canon is brief:

1592 Latin verses before William Thorne, *Tullius (STC* 24042)

1598 *Celestiall Elegies (STC* 21225)

1603 Manuscript verses on Raleigh's trial, 21 stanzas

1605? *Leicester's Ghost*, printed 1641

1607 Verses before Robert Stafforde, *Geographicall Description* (*STC* 23135)

The more important studies of Rogers are the following:

Sisson, C. J. "A Topical Reference in *The Alchemist.*" *Joseph Quincy Adams Memorial Studies*, pp. 739–41. Washington, D.C.: Folger Library, 1948.

Williams, F. B., Jr. "Thomas Rogers of Bryanston." *Harvard Studies and Notes in Philology* 16 (1934): 253–67.

———. "Leicester's Ghost." *Harvard Studies* 18 (1935): 271–85.

———. "Thomas Rogers as Ben Jonson's Dapper." Forthcoming in the *Yearbook of English Studies*.

THE TEXT: SOURCES, EDITORIAL PRINCIPLES

Leicester's Ghost survives in a long version, represented by one imperfect manuscript, and in a popular abridgment found in three seventeenth-century manuscripts and two 1641 editions. All have been collated for this edition.

R. Here designated the Rogers manuscript, MS. Additional 12132 was presented to the British Museum on 30 July 1841 by the bookseller S. Leigh Sotheby (prior provenance unknown). It contains the sole evidence of authorship, reinforced by the poet's statement (fol. 1): "Ce liure appartient a moy Thomas Rogers Angleis." In its present imperfect state it consists of 27 folio leaves, misarranged when bound. Comparison with other texts and internal evidence indicate that present folios 16–19 should follow 26 in the order 18, 17, 16, 19. It is written five stanzas to the page in a nervous but legible hand, dominantly secretary but with italic influence apart from italics for proper names. It is a highly accurate fair copy, possibly holograph, but if holograph, not rechecked or corrected by the poet. It is the only known manuscript of the original or long version, and thus is unique authority for the preliminaries and stanzas 132, 155–83, and 213–314. Since *R* lacks stanzas 51–128, it is clear that at least eight leaves have been lost between present folios 7–8. However, since the manuscript has ten stanzas to the leaf, one must conclude that at least two stanzas are irretrievably lost. *R* lacks line 943; the scribe also missed lines 68 and 1921–22, but inserted them interlinearly or in margin. The unique prelims, all in elegant italic except the epistle, collate: fol. 1, note of ownership; 1ᵛ, title; 2, prose epistle; 2ᵛ, sonnet dedication. The few scattered marginalia are described later.

P. MS. Y 185–L53 in the Newberry Library, Chicago, was formerly MS. 8990 in the library of Sir Thomas Phillipps, who bought it of dealer Thomas Thorpe in 1836. It had been lot 8714 in the 1807 sale of the library of Isaac Reed, whose endpaper signature of 1779 is the earliest provenance. The poem is written six stanzas to the page on sixteen unnumbered leaves (16ᵛ blank), in a small secretary hand of unusual beauty. A calligrapher rather than a scholar, the copyist made some stupid errors, such as "wise" rather than "wifes uncle" (line 288). His *u* often resembles *n*, particularly in the combination *un*, so that it is easy to misread *Hnnsdon* (line 297n) or *Clandius* (line 316). The text of 182 stanzas represents the first stage in the abridgment. Most of stanzas 1 and 7 are illegible from damage and stain. The scribe omitted lines 32, 418, and 531–32, and was unable to read most of 308. The chief feature of interest is the full set of marginal notes reproduced in this edition.

T. MS. Tanner 306 is a folio collection of seventeenth-century texts in several languages that came to the Bodleian Library by the will of the antiquarian Bishop Thomas Tanner (1674–1735). Academic in interest, the 158 items in the collection derive from Oxford students. The *Ghost* occupies folios 193–209ᵛ, five or six stanzas to the page. *T* has the same 182 stanzas as *P* and half its marginalia. Indeed it is a somewhat later copy in a legible italic hand of a manuscript similar to *P* (like *P* it lacks line 32, but it preserves 418 missing in *P*). Parts of lines 67–70 are lost through paper damage. In copying the concluding sonnet, the scribe transposed 5–6.

X. A second Oxford manuscript is Christ Church MS. ΣX 15A5, which was formerly the only manuscript piece in a folio volume of Restoration printed tracts (item 15 of 28). In recent times it was extracted and placed in a wrapper. The provenance is unknown; the volume was apparently at Christ Church by 1800. Lacking title and marginalia, the poem has seven stanzas to the page on thirteen numbered leaves (13ᵛ blank). The hand is rather late, small, neat, mixed italic and secretary. Unreliable as an authority, it has two points of interest. It is the sole manuscript of the final abridgment used in editions *AB;* were it not for unique substitute couplets at 412–13 and 447–48, one might suspect that it was copytext or derived from them. The couplets are probably the scribe's invention when his original was undecipherable. *X* lacks conclusion line 8. The second feature of interest is "The Supplement of this Legend" at the foot of fol. 13, a prose account of the poisoning of Leicester by his wife. This has been known from Philip Bliss's transcript in his edition of Wood's *Athenae Oxonienses* (2:74–75); Bliss noted the source only as a college library. Since the Bliss text has been used by modern writers like Elizabeth Jenkins in *Elizabeth and Leicester*, it is well to point out two flaws in this transcript: Bliss *omits* an obscure dating of the information and *misreads* the name of the informant, creating a mythical Leicester servant Haynes in place of a known William Poynes or Poyntz (see note to line 1999).

A. LEYCESTERS | GHOST. | [ornament between rules] | Printed in the yeare, | 1641.   Wing L970; cf. 968.
   Quarto in 4s: [A1], title, verso blank; A2–E3, text paged 1–35; E4 blank, often missing.
   Occasionally found alone, the *Ghost* is normally appended to the matching 1641 edition of the *Commonwealth* (Wing L968). It was set from a manuscript similar to *X.* The

routine press corrections are ignored in the apparatus; samples are: line 122 brane / braue, 296 Ceraw / Carew. The Folger copy was used in the collation, but a Harvard copy with uncorrected readings was also studied (new shelf-mark *EC A100.584cb[B]). The text is in roman, names in italic, five stanzas to the full page. It lacks lines 187 and 418, and mislocates lines 388 and 1052.

B. The page-by-page octavo reprint of the same year made some emendations from a manuscript, but its readability results from printshop care rather than textual authority. The text has been emended, with consultation of a manuscript. Though separately signatured A-B⁸, C², it is an integral part of the matching octavo *Commonwealth* (Wing L969). The press history of the first sheet is complicated. It originally began with the following titlepage [A1]:

[Row of ornaments, rule] | LEICESTER'S | GHOST. | [ornament between rules] | Printed, *Anno Dom.* MDCXLI.

For economy the text ran A1ᵛ–C2ᵛ, but extant pagination 1–34 starts at A2. Early in the operation it was decided to utilize A1 for a cancel *general* title page attributing *Commonwealth* authorship to Robert Parsons and advertising "Whereunto is added *Leicesters-Ghost.*" This title is normally found either in proper cancellans position facing the Marshall portrait of Leicester *or* in its production position as *Ghost* [A1].

But to achieve a blank verso for the cancel title, a page of text had to be sacrificed. Since the opening was essential, the second page was discarded. As a result the *Ghost* normally appears with stanzas 1–4 on A2, page 1, and stanzas 10–14 on A2ᵛ. Stanzas 5–9 are lost. This was just the first complication. In reimposing the outer forme to admit the cancel title, the printer pied adjoining A8ᵛ. Confused by conflicting collations of octavo edition with quarto copy, the compositor reset octavo B8ᵛ rather than quarto B4ᵛ. Before many copies were printed, the error was noticed and a resetting of octavo A8ᵛ was substituted. To summarize, a few early copies of the octavo have a full text, normal copies lack stanzas 5–9, and the limbo intermediate state also lacks stanzas 71–75 but shows 191–95 in two settings. The three known copies with *Ghost* title may be chance survivals rather than a genuine issue; only the Library of Congress copy is simple, while the other two are sophisticated show-pieces. The Bodleian copy (now Arch A.f.50) contains three states of A2^v, which was apparently disturbed when A8^v was pied. Two complete *Ghost* texts, with both title pages and scarce limbo A8^v, are found in the Bliss-Huth copy collated for this edition. In it Philip Bliss penned a partial collation of MS. *X*. Currently the editor's, this Huth copy will henceforth be available to scholars at Harvard. The textual variants in the states of sheet A are of no importance; the most curious is the misreading *Iustice* for *Iupiter* in line 64 (limbo state).

The text of this edition is a conflation of the author's manuscript of the long version with the stanzas lost from that manuscript but extant in the abridgment. The resulting 314 stanzas are provided with stanza and line numbers by the editor. The contents of the sources may be reviewed statistically. Sole authority for the preliminaries and 132 stanzas, MS. *R* has physically lost stanzas 51–128. The chief abridgment, represented by MSS. *P* and *T*, eliminates stanzas 132, 155–83, and 213–314. The final retouching found in MS. *X* and editions *A* and *B* further deletes stanzas 39 and 136–46. From printing accidents, nearly all copies of *B* lack stanzas 5–9 and a few lack 71–75. All texts have the concluding sonnet.

Inevitably MS. *R* is copytext, both because of its superior reliability and for its unique portions. MS. *P* is chosen as copytext for material lost from *R*, partly because it is a conscientious early transcript and partly because it has a full set of marginalia. The apparatus cites symbols in the order of the preceding descriptions, namely *RPTXAB*. The hyphenated symbol *T-B* indicates agreement in the sequence *TXAB* with the accidentals of *T*. Substantive variants occur at perhaps a thousand places. The vast majority are scribal or compositorial corruptions, pointless changes in word order, or neutral variants like the/that or ye/you. The editor has used his judgment in presenting only variants of literary interest or factual conflict. These naturally include readings illustrating the evolution of the text (e.g., the few updatings in XAB). Scribal blunders are sparingly exemplified; samples of egregious readings omitted from the apparatus are: X44 chin-falling, A293 Hampton, B409 Tarsus, X668 Hammos, B787 Pope, T892 Oxford Sheyre, T1042 Mary, P1345 Eliogatilus, A1394 Ventillius, P1440 sallow paces. Editorial policy is conservative. A census of true emendations is limited to lines 599, 1550, 2030 and 2132 (borderline at 1578, 1844, 2072). Scholars may be interested in readings at 191, 322, 375, 485, 534 and 655. Except at line 85, the authority of R is usually upheld against agreement of all other sources (as at 191, 255, 349, 897, 1319, 1408—some authorial changes?).

The copytext is transcribed *literatim* except for substitution of short for long s and departures noted in the apparatus. The manuscript use of $u|v|V$ approximates Elizabethan printing practice, though with occasional internal v. The problem of i/j does not arise, since apart from a doubtful instance at R7, the long form does not occur in the copytext. The scribes use various forms of I/J without distinction; all are transcribed as I. Original corrections and deletions are honored without notice in the apparatus. Lines overlooked but then interlined or margined are not noted in the apparatus but have been listed in the manuscript descriptions. Standard abbreviations and contractions are silently expanded. The former are expanded as: *and, our, that, the, with, which, your.* The latter are the familiar letter modifications or strokes that expand as *er, m/n, ment, per, pre, pro, us.* The downward terminal loop that other scribes use for either *-s* or *-es* is read as *-s* (in R it is rare except after terminal t, but note line 2). When obvious scribal slips are corrected, the apparatus notes only the copytext error: it may be assumed that the correction is supported by the other texts. A few scribal oversights in linear indentation and noncapitalization are silently normalized.

[[*x x i i*]]

Introduction

Thus editorial policy sanctions awkward spellings like *princly*, vacillation between *frind/freind/friend*, and an annoying confusion of *of/off*, *to/too* and *on/one*. In fact there are just two normalizations of spelling, both in stanzas from *P*. To conform with *R* usage, *spirit* in monosyllabic rhyme position is printed as *sprite*, and *exorcize* is differentiated from *exercize* (the only form known to *P-B*).

Punctuation is handled inconsistently but rationally. Except in a few stretches toward the end, *R* is liberally punctuated. Though the scribe's notion was a proliferation of commas, his pointing is respected. Any changes or additions are noted in the apparatus. On the other hand, copytext *P* has practically no punctuation; therefore in lines 351–896 the punctuation is editorial.

As for the marginalia, only *P* has an extensive set (nearly 125 notes). Therefore copytext for all marginalia is *P*, where they are all in italic. Variants are trivial and are seldom noticed in the apparatus. MS. *R* has an embryonic set of marginalia at lines 897, 900, 932, 1009, 1016, 1097, and 1100. MS. *T* eliminates almost half of the *P* marginalia and abridges a few more; a detailed list is not justified. In addition *T* shows a few comments in a later hand; these are ignored except for two citations in the explanatory notes. No marginalia appear in *XAB*.

Leicester's   Ghost

The Right Honorable, and most magnificent
Earle of Lecesters humors, conceyts, plotts,
and policies, with his life and death, impartiallie
composed in Vearse by Thomas Rogers, Es:

Viuendum recte, tum propter plurima, tum his
Præcipuè causis, vt linguas mancipiorum
Contemnas. - - - Iuuenal. - .

A Prosopopeia of the Earle of Lecesters Ghoast.

An Epistle to the iudiciall readers.

Roome for my Lord of *Lecester*, though it be but his shad-owe: yet by this ye maye iudge what manner of man he was: Whoe if he were aliue againe would eyther winne ye with fayre words to love him, or induce ye with benefites to honor him or terrifie ye with frownes to feare him. Ye must imagine that his *Ghoast* havinge wandred about the wide worlds cir-cunference, and passed through the waues of affliction, is now ariued neare the center of great *Brittaine*, where he sees the alteration of state, and commends it, discourses of his for-tune, and laments it, heares obiections opposd against him, and answeres to it. His life (too bitterly published in prose) is heare indifferently composed in vearse: not to feede the fancie of a freind that through affection would iudge partial-ly, nor to sooth the humor of a foe, that for some privat grudge would censure malitiously. Breefly I saye hee was a rare politician, I will not say a Machavellian, courteous in behavior, affable in speech, magnificent in gesture, beneficiall to his true frends, dreadfull to his prowd enemies, in freind-shipp vncertaine, in Councell secret, in revenge implacable, an Imperious Subiect, in conceyt a kinge, coueteous of glorie, greedie of others wealth, in his life highly magnified, after his Death of fewe lamented, ignoblely buried, and too soone for-gotten. Whoe if his heroicall vertues had not beene ouer-whelmed with insatiable ambition, might haue beene worthe-ly reputed one of the most excellent Courtiers in the World.

14 homor *R.*   19 secrt, *R.*   23–24 ouerwhel *R* (*margin frayed*).

〖*3*〗

The Earle of Lecesters Ghoast.

The Ghoasts speach dedicatorie to Kinge
Ieames-is most Excellent Maiestie.

Great Brittaynes Kinge, rare, puissant, opulente,
In wisedome, Empire, and your Subiects loue,
Maie I presume my shadowe to present,
To you that are Chiefe Viceroye vnder Ioue?
My Liege I come from dead mens hollowe caues,   5
With due alleageance to salute your Grace,
In spite of that foule Iaylor of mens graues,
I walke abroad, and seeke some restinge place.
To whome, but to your Highnes should I come?
Vnder whose pasport I maye safely passe,   10
Althoughe my corpes be banisht by Heavens doome,
Behould my figure in this tragic glasse.
  Dread Lord, then bid me welcome to your shore,
  That if I liud, would now your Grace adore.

In Zoilum Distichon.   15

Si imbellis placeat bello Regi iste Libellus,
  Nil curo si in me (Zoile) bella geris.

The Earle of Lecesters Ghoast.

I that sometime shin'd like the Orient Sun,
Though *Fortuns* Subiect, yet a puissant Lord,
Am now an Obiect to be gazd vppon,
An Abiect rather, fitt to be deplord,
Deiected nowe, that whilom was adord,   5
 Affected once, suspected since of manye,
 Reiected now, respected scarce of anye.

My Spirit hou'ringe in the foggie ayre,
Since it did pass the frozen *Stygian* flood,
Vnto great *Brittaynes* Empire did repayre,   10
Where of *Elisaes* death I vnderstood,
And that the *Heav'ns* carefull of *Englands* good,
 Raysd vp a Kinge, who crownd with love and peace,
 Brings in newe ioyes, and makes old griefs to cease.

Thus from the Concaue vaults of starr-lesse Night,   15
Where neuer Sun, nor Moone vouchsaft to shine,
My wretched *Ghoast* is come at length to light,
By Charter graunted from the Power divine,
Snake-eating Envye, O doe not repine
 At honors Shadow, doe not bite the dead,   20
 My pride is past, my pompe from th' earth is fled:

Title RP] The Earle of *om. TAB, none X.*   1 Sun *R*   14
Brings . . . makes *RPT*] Brought . . . made *XAB.*   20
Shadow *R.*

My princly byrth, my high-ennobled state,
My sometime dreadfull frownes nowe none regard,
My great good turnes to many donne of late,
With greatfull harts now fewe or none reward,   25
My *Fame* is blotted out, my *Honor* scard,
   My Monuments defac'd, my Reliques torne,
   Yea Vassals doe my Excellency scorne.

Ah sylly Pesants, as each Grecian Boy,
Would brave stout *Hector*, being dead and cold,   30
That whilom was the *Piller* of ould Troye,
Whose presence living they durst scarce behold,
Soe since ye see me dead, ye grow soe bould,
   As to controll my acts, whose lookes did daunt
   The proudest Peare that liud in Troynouant.   35

A tyme there was when stately *Bears* could climbe,
And in that time was I a stately Beare;
Who climbed vp so fast in little tyme,
That other beasts did my highe-mounting feare,
My Fortunes by theire downfall I did reare,   40
   I ioy enioyd, whilst I made others mourne,
   And serud the *Tyme*, to make *Tyme* serue my tourne.

I was the Ofspring of a Princely Syre,
He too well knowne by his climb-falling pride,
Like *Dædalus* did teach me to aspire,
We both did fly, he fell, I did but slide,
Like in attempts, yet vnlike chance we tryde,
   He by a *Queene* did dye, but as it chanced,
   I by a *Queene* did liue, and was advanced.

Iohn Duke of
Northumberland
Father to my Lo:
of Leicester be-
headed in Queene
Maries time and
his sonne ad-
uaunced by
Queene Elizabeth.

Periods supplied at 35, 42, 49.   43n *Mislocated at* 36 *in PT.*
47 attemps, *R.*

[8]

For Lady *Iane* by him a *Queene* Proclaymd   50
Was soone supprest, *Queene Mary* got the Crowne,
Which as her proper right she boldly claymd,
My Father striued in vayne to keepe her downe,
And for that, lost his life, I my renowne,
   Till sacred *Cynthia* to the Kingdome came   55
   That gaue new life to my late-dying *Fame:*

That peerless *Queene* of happy Memorye,
Who late like *Deborah* this Kingdome swayd,
Now tryvmphes in the Iasper colourd skye,
In Starr-embroydred vesture richly rayd,   60
She, She restord my *Honor* then decayd,
   When *Treason* did attaynt my *Fathers* blood,
   And drownd our Princly race in *Lethes* flood.

Then Iupiter was in my Horoscope,   The Earle of
And *Cynthia* blest me with her fayre aspect,   Lecesters riseinge
What myght not then my youth and courage hope,
When me my *Souueraigns* fauor did protect,
O what may not a *Princes* grace effect,
   When Maiesty on haplesse men doth smile,
   Whose Ioyes did seeme to perish in exile.   70

Euen when Queene Maryes tragic raigne did ende,
My comic Fortune in the prime begunne,
That tyme when *Cynthias* brightness did extend,
To lighten this darke land, whose splendent *Sun*
Was in *Eclypse,* and sorrowes streames did runn,   75
   I like the glorious day-starre did appeare,
   With fayre vprize to grace this *Hemispheare.*

[9]

Since Brute first swayd this all-vnited land,
Noe subiect firmer held his Souueraignes grace,
My will Imperiall for a *Lawe* did stand,
Such was my *Princes* pleasure, such my place,
As *Momus* durst not offer me disgrace;
    What man did smile, when *Lesters* browe did frowne,
    Whose witt could guide, though neuer get, the crowne.

Brute the firste Kinge of Albion

80

Whilest in this glorious *Ocean* I did swimme,
To high preferment divers men I brought,
Which since haue sought my honors lampe to dimme,
Yea such as I before advancd of nought
Against my person trecheries haue wrought.
    Thus *Honors* doe oftimes good manners change,
    And men growne rich, to aintient freinds grow strainge.

The ingratitude of some towards the Earle of Lecester

90

I greiue to thinke I did such men advance,
And rayse their base lines to a stately pitch,
Vnder the shadowe of my countenance,
The substance of the *Earth* did make them ritch,
What furie did their sences thus bewitch?
    Or was it some ill spirit that possest them,
    To seeke my ruine, whose large bounty blest them?

95

Thus they in vayne my downefall did conspire,
Like Doggs that at the *Moone* doe fondly barke,
And did but burne themselues like *Ætnas* fyre,
Or like grimme Oules did wander in the darke,
Contemnd of me, who mounted like the Larke,
    Or that rare Bird that builds his nest on highe
    In *Cædar* trees, whose topps affront the skie.

100

105

85 glorious *P-B*] glories *R tampered.*   *Periods supplied at* 89, 105.   104 his *RPTA*] her *XB.*

When I commaunded, who durst countermaund;
Were not meane Subiects subiect to my becke?
What man of woorth my pleasure did withstand;
What simple swaines could doe, I did not recke,
I gaue the Mate to those that gaue me checke,   110
　　By the *Queenes* helpe, my power, and threatning looks
　　I ruld the Pawnes, the Bishops, Knights, and Rookes.

Thus did I play at Chesse, and wanne the game,
Having the *Queene* my puissaunce to support,
The Bishops for Ambition did me blame,   115
The Pawnes affirmd I wanne by much extort,
The Rookes and Knights found draughts to marre my
　　　　sport:
　　Had not some stopt me with their timely checks,
　　I might haue giuen them Check without their necks.

My brayne had witt, my toungue was eloquent,   His excellent parts
Fit to discourse, or tell a courtly tale,
My presence portly, brave, magnificent,
My woords imperious, stout, substantiall,
My gestures loving, kind, Heroicall,
　　My thoughts ambitious, prowd and full of ire,   125
　　My deeds were good or bad, as Tymes require.

Some of my foes that bore me deadly hate,
That had to them cheefe offices assignd,
And were my fellow *Consuls* in the state,
Emulous of my still aspiring minde,   130
Gaue me this prayse (though otherwise vnkind)
　　That I was wonndrous politick, and wise,
　　A statesman that knew how to temporize.

107 meane *RTXAB*] great *interlined R,* men *P in error.*   111
helpe *R.*   113 game *R.*   125 ambitious *R.*   133 temporize *R.*

[*11*]

Some others tooke me for a Zealous man,
Because good preachers I did patronize,   135
And many thought me a Precisian,
But God doth know, I neuer was precise,
I seemd devout in Godly Exercise,
     And by Religious shew confirmed my might,
     But whoe durst say, I was an *Hypocrite?*   140

As *Numa,* when he first did seeke to drawe,   Numa the second
The *Romaine* People vnderneath his yoke,   Kinge of Roome
Tuching Religion he ordeynd a lawe,   that brought the
And faynd, he with the Nymphe *Ægeria* spoke,   Romans into Ciuill
That him to this good motion did provocke,   Gouerment by
     Whereby (as if it were by heavens consent)   establishinge a
     He brought his men to Ciuill goverment.   Kinde of Religion.
         Plutarch in vita
         Numa Pompil.

Soe when I came in high affayres to deale,
Of sound Religion I did make a showe,
And by pretence of hott and fervent Zeale   150
In welth and faction I more stronge did growe,
For this by practize I did playnly know,
     That men are apt to yeald to any motion
     Made by a man that is of pure devotion.

Yet could I strayne my conscience for a neede,   155
For though I seemd an earnest protestant,
For gaine I favour Papists: soe indeede
Some held me for a Newter, and I graunt,
To serue my tourne, I could turne Puritant.
     Thus by Religion honor some doe winne,   160
     And this fayre Cloake oft couers filthy sinne:

139 might *R.*   159 Puritant *R.*

Like as the ayre-sucking *Chamælion*
Can him transforme to any hue saue white,
Soe man can turne to any fashion,
Saue to that forme which is syncere, and right,   165
For though he may delude the Peoples sight,
  It is in vayne before God to dissemble,
  Whose power the Diuells know, and knowing tremble.

Was I the only man that haue offended
In making holynes a cloake for sinne?   170
The Frenchmen for Religions sake pretended,
Their ciuill wars of late tyme did beginne,
But yet Ambition cheefely drew them in,
  Yea madd Ambition and desire of gaine,
  Makes endless broyles betwixt the States and Spaine.   175

Of promises I was so prodigall,   His Lardge prom-
So kind, well-spoken, and soe politick,   ises to the Clargy
That to some great Diuine (as it might fall)
Perhaps I promised a Bishopricke,
Yet in performance I was nothing quicke,   180
  Thus with fayre words mens humors oft I fed,
  Whilst Hope this while a good Opinion bred.

To learned Schollers I was somewhat francke,   His inclinacion to
Not for the love that I to learning bore,   Schollers in gen-
But either to get prayse or picke a thanke   erall
Of such as could the Muses ayd implore,
To consecrate my name for euermore,
  For he is blest that soe befrended dies,
  Whose prayse the Muses will immortalize.

166 thought *R.*   167 dissemble *R.*

Ye that desire to haue your fame surviue,   190
When ye within your graues inhum'de shall ly,
Cherish those sacred Sisters while ye liue,
For they be Daughters of Dame Memory,
And of the thundring Monarch of the skye,
    They have the guift to register with penn,   195
    Th' eternall fame, or infamy of men.

The students of the Vniversitie,   *Chauncellor of*
Oxford whereof I was the *Chancelour*,   *Oxford*
That *Nource of Science* and *Philosophie*,
Knowing the greatnes of my witt, and power,   200
Did honor me as the fayre springing flower,
    That in the Princes favor highly grew,
    Whome shee with showers of gould did oft bedewe.

At my commaund both *Dee*, and *Alin* tended,   *Doctor Dee and*
By magic art my pleasure to fullfill,   *Alline of*
These to my service their best studies bended,   *Glocesters Hall*
Any why? they durst not disobeye my will,
Yea whatsoeuer was of secret skill,
    In *Oxford*, or in *Camebridge* to be sould,
    I gott for love, for feare, or els for gould.   210

Doubtless the most renownd *Philosophers*,   *Cornelius Agrippa*
As *Plato*, and *Pythagoras* haue sought   *de occulta Philo-*
To learne the *Hieroglific Characters*,   *sophia*
And secrets which by *magic* skill are wrought,
Such as th *Ægyptians*, *Iewes*, and *Caldees* tought.   215
    Th' art is not ill, if men doe not abuse it,
    Noe fault soe bad, but some man will excuse it.

191 inhum'de *R*] intombd *P-B*.   202 grew *R*.   210 gould
R.   215 tought *R*.

Lopus and *Iulio* were my cheif *Phisitions*,　　　　　
Men that were cuning in the *Art* to kill,
Good *Schollers*, but of passing ill conditions,　　　　220
Such as could rid mens liues yet noe blood spill,
Yea with such great dexteritie and skill
　　Could giue a dramme of poyson that should slay,
　　At end of th' yeare, the month, the weeke or day.

I never did the wicked men imploye,　　　　225
To wrong my *Prince* or my true loving freind,
But false deceitfull wretches to destroye,
And bring them to an vnexpected end,
Let them looke to it that did most offend,
　　Whose names are registred in Plutoes schroles,　　　230
　　For I will neuer answere for their soules.

Knights, and Esquires, the cheif in euery sheire,　　　
Did wayt one me through *England* vp and downe,
And some amonge them did my liuerie weare,
My smiles did seeme to promise them renowne,　　　235
But dismal haps ensud when I did frowne,
　　As when the starr *Arctûrus* doth appeare,
　　Of raging tempests sea-men stand in feare.

As for the *Souldiers* and the men of warre,　　　Captaines and
At home in service some I did reteyne,　　　　souldiers main-
Others I sent abroad, not very farre,　　　　tained by the Earle
At my commandment to retorne againe,　　　　of Lecester.
These I with cost did secretly mainteyne,
　　That if ought chanc'd me otherwise then well,
　　I might haue sent my foes to *Heauen* or *Hell*.　　　245

235 renowne *R*.　　239 warre *R*.

[*15*]

Likewise I brought the *Lawyers* in some awe,   His Authoritie
The worthy students of the *Inns of Court*,   amongst the
                                                       Lawiers
That then applyd them to the *Common Lawe*,
Did yeald to me in matters of import,
Although sometime I did the lawe extort,   250
    And whether right, or wronge, my case once heard,
    To plead against me, made great *Lords* affeard.

Soe the *Lord Barkly* lost good land by might,
Whereof perhaps at first he did not dreame,
Might many times doth overthrowe the right,   255
It is in vayne to striue against the streame,
When he that is cheif Subiect in the Reame,
    Vppon his princes favor beares him bould,
    He cannot, or he will not be contrould.

Thus by the *Queene* my puissance was vpheld,   His power by the
And for my foes I euer was to stronge,   Queens fauour
The grace I had from her, all feare expeld,
I might wronge others, but not suffer wronge,
Soe many men did vnto me belonge,
    Which on my fauour chiefly did depend,   265
    And for my sake, bothe goods, and blood would spend.

About the *Queene* such Creatures I did place,
Whose service I approved firme, and true,
Such Ladies did attend vppon her *Grace*,
As I presented to her *Highness* viewe,   270
Whose harts to me assurd in love I knew,
    Thus fewe things at the *Court* by day were donne,
    But I did know, ere Titans race was runne.

251 case *R*] cause *P-B*.   255 overthrowe *R*] ouercome *P-B*.

The best esteemed Nobles of this land
On whose support the *Publike* state relied,
Were linckt with me in freindshipps faythfull band,
Or els in kindred nearely were allied,
Their perfect love and constant harts I tried,
  Th' inferiour sort at our devotion stood,
  Ready to execute what we thought good.

His great Alliaunce
and faction

280

The *Earle* of Warwicke my owne loving Brother,
My Sisters Husband th' *Earle* of Huntington,
The bounteous *Earle* of Bedford was another
Of my best freinds, beloud of everyone,
Sir Henry Sydneis power in *Wales* well knowne,
  And there the *Earle of Pembrooke* chief of all,
  Of kinne, my frends, what euer chance might fall.

His power in Wales

In *Barwicke* my wiefs Vncle had cheefe power,
The *Lord of Hunsdon* my assured freind,
In Ireland the *Lord Graye* was governor,
Gernsey, and *Gersey* likewise did depend,
Vppon such men as did my will attende,
  Hopton my man, Liuetenant of the *Tower*,
  Was prompt to doe me service at an hower.

In Barwicke

Ireland

Gernsay

Sir Owen Hopton
my Lord of Leces-
ters seruant Lieu-
tenant of the Tower

Sir Edward Horsey in the *Isle of Wight*,
And noble *Sir Georg Carye* next bore swaye,
Men of great courage, and noe little might,
To take my part in any doubtfull fray,
In *London* the Recorder *Fleetwood* laye
  That often vsd good woords which might incence
  The *Citizens* to stand in my defence.

Sir Edward Horsey

Sir George Cary
late Lo: of Huns-
don

The Record-
er Fleetwood

280 good *R.*   289 *Hunsdon P-B*] *Hundsdon R.*   294 hower *R.*   301 defence *R.*

[*17*]

The Prentises did likewise take my part,
As I in private quarrels often tryde,
Soe that I had the very head and hart,
The *Court* and *Citty* leaning one my side,   305
With flattery some, others with guifts I plide,
    And some with threats, stearne looks, and angry words,
    I woone to my defence with clubbs and swords.

Thus I by wisdome and fine policie,
Mayntaynd the reputation of my life,   310
Drawing to me the flower of Chivalrey,
To succor me at neede in ciuill strife,
Men that loud chainge in every place were rife,
    And all the *Realme* was with my power possest:
    Thinke what this might haue wrought but iudge the
      best.   315

Like *Claudius Marcellus* drawne through *Rome*,
In his fayre Charriot with rich Trophees deckt,
Crowned with garlands by the *Senats* doome,
Whom they fiue times their *Consul* did elect,
That from their foe he might their liues protect,   320
    When he with conquest did his country greet,
    Load with rich spoyles, layd prostrat at his feet.

Soe did I ride in trivmphe through cheife Townes
As if I had been *Vice-roye* of this land,
My face well grac'd with smiles, my purse with crownes,   325
Holding the raynes of honnor in my hand,
I managed the state, I did commaund,
    My looks with humble Maiestie repleat,
    Made some men wish me a kings royall seate.

314 possest *R.*   315 iudg *R;* best *R frayed.*   316 *Mareellus*
R.   322 Load . . . rich *R-X*] Loads of rich *A*, Loaden with
B; layd *RPT*] lay *XAB;* feet, *R.*   324 been, *R.*

Thus waxt I popular to purchace Fame,   His Popularitie
To me the common *Peoples* knees did bowe,
I could my humor still soe fittly frame
To enterteyne all men (to outward showe)
With inward love, for few my hart did knowe,
    And that I might not seeme puft vp with pride,   335
    Bareheaded oft through Citties I did ride.

While some cryde out, God saue you, Gratious Lord,
Lord! how they did my fame hyperbolize,
My words and gestures did soe well accord,
As with their harts they seemd to sympathize,   340
I charmd their eares, and did enchaunt their eyes,
    Thus was I reckned their cheefe *Potentate*,
    No poler, but a piller of the state.

Then was I cald the Hart, and Life of the Courte,   He was called the
And some (I wott) wisht I had binne the head,   Harte and life of
I had soe great a trayne, and such a port,   the Courte
As did the Pompe of Mortimer exceede,
Who (as in th' *English Chronicles* we read)
    When Second Edward lost his kingly *rites*,
    Was wayted on at once with nine score knights.   350

The *Earle of March, Sir Roger Mortimer*,   A Comparison be-
Ruld the younge Kinge, Queene Mother and the Peeres.   twixte the Earle of
I, *Robert Dudley, Earle of Lecester*,   March and the
Did swaye in Courte and all the *English* Sheires.   Earle of Leicester
His rule was shorte; myne florish'd many yeres.   355
    He did his life with ignominie loose;
    I liu'd and tryumph'd ouer my proudest foes.

337 you *R.*   338 Lord; *R.*   349 *rites R*] rights *P-B.*
351–896 *missing from R; text follows P, with punctuation edi-*
torial.   356 ignomine *P.*

As th' Image of great *Alexander* dead
Made King *Cassander* tremble at the sight,
Spying the figure of his royall head   360
Whose presence sometymes did the world affright,
Or like as *Ceasars* monarchising sprite
    Pursu'd false *Brutus* at *Phillippoes* feild
    Till he that slew his liege himselfe had killd;

Soe view (ye Pettie Lords) my princely ghoast.   His speech to such
I speake to yow whose harts were full of gall.   of the Nobilitie and
I whilst I liu'd was honored of the most,   loued him not.
And ether feard for loue of greate and smale,
Or lou'd for feare of such as wisht my fall.
    Behold my shaddowe, representing state,   370
    Whose person sometymes did your pride abate.

Wheigh what I was, Knights, Gentlemen and Peeres,
When my death-threatening frownes did make ye quake.
As yet there hath not passed many yeeres
Since I your plumes pluckt, loftie chrests did shake.   375
Then tell me, Sirs, for old acquaintance sake,
    Waxe ye not pale to here of Lecesters name,
    Or to backbyte him blush ye not for shame?

Ye saie that I in dealings was vniust,   The obiection of
As if true iustice ballance ye could guide.   his iniustice
Had I dealt iustly, I had turn'd to dust
Long before this your corpes swolne vp with pride,
Which nowe surviueing, doe my Acts deride:
    My fame yet lives, though death abridg'd my daies;
    Some of you dy'd that overlyud your praise.   385

362 sprite *R spelling at* 957 *etc.*] spirit *PT*, spright *XAB*.
365n to *om. P.*   375 plumes *XAB*] plume *PT;* shake *XAB*]
strake *PT.*

Are there not some among you Parasites?

The Answere

Tyme seruers and obseruers of noe measure?
Prince smoothers, people pleasers, hipocrits?
Damn'd Machauillians giuen to lust and pleasure,
Church Robbers, beggars of the Princes Treasure?

390

  Trucebreakers, Pyrats, Athiests, Sycophants?
  Can equitie dwell here where conscience wants?

And yet yow thinke none iustly deales but yow!

Astrea the God-
desse of Iustice
fayned by the Poets
to be turned into
one of the twelue
signes called Libra

Devyne *Astrea* vp to heaven is fled
And turn'd to *Libra;* there looke vpp and viewe
Her ballance in the *Zodiack* figured.
Iust *Aristides* once was banished:

Aristides a iust man
banished by the
Lawe of ostracisnon
through enuy Plut.
in vita. Aris.

  Where liues his match whome *Enuy* did pursue
  Because men thought he was to iust and true?

Ye saie ambicion harbored in my braine?

The obiections of
his Ambition

I saie Ambition is noe haynous synne;
To men of State doe Statly thoughts perteine—
By baser thoughts what honor can ye winne?
Who ever did a greate exployt beginn
  Before Ambition mou'd him to the deede   405
  And hope of honor vrged him to proceede?

Themistocles had never put to flight

The Answere

Xerxes huge hoast or tam'd the *Persians* pride,
Nor had King *Pyrrhus* gott by martiall fight
The Romans spoiles with conquest on his side,

410

If first Ambicion had not beene theire guide:
  Had not this humor theire stoute harts allured
  To high attempts, theire fame had beene obscured.

394 *and* 394n Austrea *P.*   397n Aristippus *P.*   402
thought *P.*   408 *Xexes P.*   412–13 *X substitutes:* Ambition is the foode which honor finds / In greate attempts to
feede asspiring minds.

The *Eagle* doth disdaine to catch small flies,
The *Lyon* with the *Ape* doth scorne to play,   415
The *Dolphin* doth the *Whirlpooles* loue despise:
Thus yf Birds, Beasts, and Fishes beare such swaye
As yf they would teach vnderlings to obay,
   Much more should men, whome reason doth adorne,
   Be noble mynded and base fortune scorne.   420

Admitt I could dissemble wittily—   The obiections of
This is noe grevious sinn in men of State.   his Dissimulacion
Dissembling is a point of policie;   and his answere
Plaine dealing nowe growes stale and out of date.
Wherefore I oft conceald my priuy hate   425
   Till I might find fitt tyme, though long I stayd,
   To wreake the wrath, that in my harte I lay'd.

The proverbe is, plaine dealeing is a Iewell,
But he that vseth yt a beggar dyes.
The world is noweadaies become soe crewell   430
That *Courtiers* doe plaine countrymen despise.
Quick witts and cuning heads doe quickly rise,
   And to be plaine, ye must not plainly deale
   That office seek in court or common weale.

Nowe *Aristippus* is in more request,   Aristippus a Phi-
That knewe the waye to please a Monarchs mynd,   losopher whome
Then that poore *Cynic* swad that vsed to jest   Diogenes called the
At every idle knave that he could find.   Roiall Dogg for his
To vnkind freinds ye must not be to kynd.   adullation of great
   This is a Maxime which to yow I giue: Princes Diog:
   Men must dessemble or they cannot live.   Laert:
                                                                440

416 *Whir-pooles P.*   418 *missing PA, text from T.*   420
noble *T-B*] noblye *P.*   428 The *P*] The ould *T-B.*   434
seek *TXB*] seeks *PA.*   437 *Cynie P.*   438n Dionisi: *P.*

Ye saie I was a coward in the feild?
I saie yt fitts not such a noble wight
To whome his country doth the title yeeld
Of Lord *Leuitenaunt* with full power and might   445
To venture his owne person in the fight.
  Let others dye, that as our Vassalls serue,
  Whilst heaven to better haps our hopes reserue.

The obiection of
his want of vallour

Howe soone did Englands ioye in Fraunce diminish
When the *Earle of Salisbury* at *Orleaunce*   450
By gunshott strooke his honord life did fynish?—
When *Talbott,* that did often times advance
The English Ensignes in disgrace of Fraunce
  Was at the last environed and slaine,
  Whose name the Frenchmens terror doth remaine.   455

And what a fatall wound did Rome receiue
By Crassus death, whome Faithlesse *Partheans* slewe!
Howe did the Senate for Flaminius greiue,
And for *Æmylius* death and his stoute crewe,
Which *Hannyball* at *Cannes* did subdue:
  Cut off an Arme, yet life the harte maye cherrish;
  Cutt off the head, and every parte will perishe.

Plutarch in vita
Crassus:

Idem in vita
Hanniball Idem
in vita Æmyl:

Iphycrates the *Athenian* vsed to saie
Vaunt-Currers are like hands to battaile prest,
The men of Armes as feete whereon to staye,   465
The footmen as the Stomacke and the brest,
The Captaine as the head aboue the rest:
  The head, once crased, troubleth all the parts;
  The generall, slaine, doth kill Tenn thowsand harts.

447–48 X *substitutes:* The man whose life to many liues giues
breath / Not rashly should expose himselfe to death.   448
haps *AB*] hopes *P,* hapes *corrected to* hopes *T.*   456 Rome
T-B] *blank in P.*   457 Crasus *P.*   458 Flammius *P.*
460 at *T-B*] to *P.*

Therefore a lord *Leuitenant* should take care   470
That he himself in saftie doe repose
And should not hazard life at euery dare,
But watch and ward: so *Fabius* tyrd his foes,
When rash *Minutius* did the conquest loose.
    If such in open Dainger will intrude,   475
    Yt is fond rashnes and not fortitude.

Ye saie I was Lasciuious in my love   The obiections of
And that I tempted many a gallant Dame;   his Lasciuiousnes
Nor soe content, but I did often prove   in Loue
To wynn theire handmaids if I lik'd the game.   480
Why, Sirs, yow knowe love kyndles such a flame,   His answere
    As if we maye beleeue what *Poets* penn,
    It doth incense the harts of Gods and men.

Ioue lou'd the daughter of a Iealous Sire,
Danae a mayde imur'd within a Tower,   485
Yet to accomplish th' end of his desire,
He, metamorphoz'd to a golden shower,
Fell in the Lapp of his Deere *Parramoure*,
    And being tearmed a God, did not disdaine
    To turne a man, a beast, a shower of rayne.   490

Deere lords, when *Cupid* throwes his fyrie Darts,
Doth none of them your tender bodies hitt?
Doth *Cytherea* never charme your harts,
Nor beavtie trye your quintessentiall witt?
Perhapps yow will saie noe, fye, tis vnfitt!   495
    Now by my Garter and my *George* to boote,
    The blind God surly hitts yf once he shoote.

475 an *P*.   485 Danae a mayde *X-B*] Dana amid *PT*.

Whereas ye doe obiect by magic charmes
I sought to winn faire Dames to my desire,
Tis better soe then striue by force of Armes,
For forced love will quickly back retyre.
Yf faire meanes cannot wyn what we require,
  Some tricks and secrett slights must be devised
  That love may even from Hell be exorcized.

The obiection of
his practices by
art magic

To your dull witts it seemes impossible
By drinks and charmes this worke to passe to bring?
Knowe then that *Giges* went invisible
By turning of the sigil of his ring
Towards his palme, and thereby slewe the kinge,
  Lay with his wife of any man vnseene,
  Lastly did raigne by marrying with the Queene.

505
Plato makes men-
tion of this Giges

Kinge Candaules
that shewed his
wife naked to this
Giges was after-
wards slaine by
both theire con-
sents

King *Solamon* for magic naturall
Was held a cuning man by some deuines;
He wrote a booke of sciens misticall
To bynd ill spirits in theire darke confines.
He had great store of wiues and concubines,
  Yet was a sacred king: thus I inferr
  The wisest man that now doth live may err.

His wisdome ex-
ceeded the Cal-
deans and south-
saiers 2 booke of
the Kings
Iosephus affirmeth
that he wrote a
booke to binde and
charme Devils and
ill spirits

Alsoe ye saie that when I waxed old,
When age and time misspent had made me dry—
For auncient eld in carnall lust is cold—
Natures defect with Arte I did supplie,
And that to helpe this imbecilitie,
  I vsd strange drinks and Oyntments of good prise,
  Whose tast or touch might make dead flesh to rise.

The obiection of
his arte to strength-
en venery

525

504 exercized *P-B; only R* (*here missing*) *distinguishes* exor-
cise/exercise.   520 mispent *P.*   521 eld *P*] held *TAB; X
substitutes:* And that through years my . . .   523 to helpe
XA] the people *P;* did helpe *TB.*

To this I answered that those fine extractions,

His answere and defence

Drammes and electuaries rarely made
Serv'd not soe much to help veneriall actions
As for to comfort nature that decay'd;
Which being with indifferent iudgment waigh'd,   530
   In noble men may bee alowd (I trust)
   As lending to their health, not to theire lust.

What if I dranke nothing but Liquid Gold,
Lachryma Christi, pearle resolued in wyne,
Such as the full *Egiptians* cupps did hold   535
When *Cleopatra* with her lord did dyne?
A trifle, care not, for the cost was myne.
   What yf I gaue Hippomanes in drinke
   To some faire Dames? at smale faults ye must wincke.

Ye saie I was a Traytor to the Queene?

The obiection of his discontent and inclinacion to rebellion in Mounsieurs time

And that when *Mounsieur* was in greatest grace,
I beeing out of fauor, mou'd with spleene
To see a Frenchman frolicke in that place,
Forth towards *Barwicke* then did post apace,
   Mynding to raise vp a rebellious route   545
   To take my parte in what I went aboute?

That I was then a Traytor I denie,

His answere and defence

But I confesse that I was *Mounsieurs* foe
And sought to breake that league of amity
Which then betweene my *Prince* and him did growe,   550
Doubting religion might be changed soe,
   Or that our lawes and customes were in danger
   To be corrupt or altred by a stranger.

531–32 *missing from P, text of X.*   534 *Lachryma* (*see notes*)]
Lactirmia P, Lactrina, T-B; Christi P] *Cristall T-B.*   536
Cleoptra P.   544 *Barwicke P-B*] *error for* Warwicke (*see notes*).   545 rebellous *P.*

Therefore I did a faction strong maintaine
Against the *Earle of Sussex*, a stoute Lord
On *Mounsieurs* side and then lord *Chamberlaine*,
Who sought to make that Nuptiall accord
Which none maye breake, wittnes the sacr'd word;
 But thus yt chaunc'd that he striued in vaine
 To knitt that knott which heaven did not ordaine. 560

Thus ye did misinterpret my conceits
That for disloyaltie my deeds did blame.
Yet manie men haue layd theire secrett baits
To entrappe me in such snares to worke my shame,
Whome I in tyme sufficientlie did tame 565
 And by my Soveraignes fauor bore them downe,
 Proveing myself true liegman to the Crowne.

Thinke ye I could forgett my Soueraigne Lady,
That was to me soe gratious and soe kynd?
How many Tryumphes for her glorye made I!
O, I could never blott out of my mynd
What characters of grace in her haue shin'd:
 But some of yow that were by her preferr'd
 Have with her bones almost her name inter'd.

When she was gone, which of yow all did weepe?
What mournfull song did *Philomela* sing?
Alas, when she in deaths cold bed did sleepe,
Which of yow all her dolefull knell did ringe?
How long will yow loue your newe crowned Kinge
 Yf yow soe soone forgett your old *Queene* dead, 580
 That fowre and fortie yeres hath gouerned?

557 Nuptiall *T-B*] mutuall *P.* 571 blott *T-B*] plott *P.*
573 was *P.* 579 loue your newe *PT*] now loue your *XAB*
modernizing.

A faction betwixt
the Earle of Sus-
sex and Lecester
aboute the mar-
riage of the Queene
with Mounsieur

His true Allea-
geance to the
Queene

He blameth some
for theire ingrati-
tude and forgetfull-
nes of soe excellent
a Prince

Ye saie I sought by murder to aspire,
And by strong poysons manie men to slaye,
Which (as ye thought) might crosse my high desire
And cloud my long expected golden daie.   585
Perhapps I laid some blocks out of my waie
   Which hindred me from comming to that Bower
   Where *Cynthia* shind like Lamps in *Pharos* Tower.

Alas, I came not of a Tygars Kynde;
My hands with blood I hated to defile,   590
But when by good experience I did find
How some with faigned love did me beguile,
Perchaunce all pittie then I did exile,
   And—as yt were against my will—was prest
   To seeke theire deathes that did my life detest.   595

Loe then, attend to here a dolefull tale   A Lamentable
Of those whose death ye doe suppose I wrought.   discourse
Yet wish I that the world beleeve not all
That hath of me by envious men beene taught,
But when I for a Kingly fortune sought,   600
   O pardon me, my self I might forgett,
   And cast downe some, my State aloft to sett.

My first wife fell downe from a paire of Staires   The death of my
And brake her necke, and soe at *Conmore* dyed;   Lo: of Lecesters
Whilst her true servants, lead with small affaires,   wife at Conmore a
Vnto a fayre at *Abbingdon* did ride,   place 4 or 5 miles
This dismall happ did to my wife betyde: from Oxford where
   Whether ye call yt chance or destinie,   this Ladie dyed
   Too true yt is she did vntimely dye.

585 could *P.*   588 *Pharos X*] *Pharoes P, Pharoos T, Pha-*
rohs, AB.   597 whose whose *P.*   599 taught *rhyme emend.*
fr. stanza 31] wrought *PTXB,* wrot *A, all for* wrote?   603
from *X-B*] *om. PT.*

Oh, had I nowe a shower of Teares to shed,   610
Lockt in the emptye circles of myne eyes!
All could I spend in mourning for the dead,
That lost a spouse soe yong, soe faire, soe wise!
Soe faire a corps, soe fowle a course nowe lyes:
   My hope to haue married with a famous *Queene*   615
   Draue pittie backe, and kept my teeres vnseene.

What man soe fond that would not lose a pearle   Quid non mortalia
To find a *Dyamond*, leaue brasse for *Gold?*   pectora cogit
Or who could not forgett a gallant gearle   Regni sacra fames
To wynn a *Queene*, greate men in awe to hold?   620
To rule the State, of none to be controwl'd:
   O but the Stepps that leade vnto a throne
   Are dangerous for men to tread vppon!

The *Cardinall Chattillian* was my foe,   The death of Car-
Whose death I peradventure did compact,   dinall Chattillian
Because he let *Queene Elizabeth* to knowe
My false reporte giuen of a former Acte—
How I with her had made a precontract,
   And the great Princes hopes I bard thereby,
   Which su'de to marrie with her Maiestye.   630

The Prelate had beene better held his tongue
And kist his holy Fathers feete in *Roome*.
A masse the sooner for his soule was sung,
But he may thanke me, had he staid at home,
Or late or never he to heaven had come: 635
   Therefore I sent him nimblye from the coasts,
   Perhapps to supper with the lord of hoasts.

614 no lyes *P*.   627 forme *P*.   628 her *T-B*] him *P*.
631 hold *P*.

When death by happ my first wifes necke had crackt
It chaunced that I made a postcontract,   640
And did in sorte the Ladie *Sheffeild* wed,
Of whome I had Twoe goodly children bred
   (For the Lord *Sheffeild* dyed, as I was sure,
   Of a Catarch which Phisick could not cure).

Some thinke the Rewme was Artificiall   645
Which this good Lord before his end did take.
Tush, what I gaue to *her* was naturall!
My plighted troth yet some amends did make,
Though her at length, vnkind, I did forsake:
   She must not blame me, for a higher reach   650
   Made my sure promise find a sodaine breach.

The valliant *Earle* whome, absent, I did wronge   The death of the
In breaking *Hyminæus* holy band,   renowned Earle of
In *Ireland* did protract the tyme too long,   Essex.
Whilst some in *England* ingled vnderhand,   655
And at his coming homeward to this land,
   He died with poison, as they saie, infected,
   Not without cause—for vengance, I suspected.

Because this fact notorious scandall bred,
And for I did his gallant wife abuse,   660
To salue the sore when this braue Lord was dead,
I for my wife did his faire Ladie chuse.
All flesh is fraile! Dere Ladie, me excuse:
   It was pure love that made me vndertake
   This happlesse recontract with thee to make.   665

640 It] I *P.*   645 Rewme *T-B*] *blank in P.*   647 *her*] her
PTXB, him *A.*   654 protect *P.*   655 ingled *PXB*] Iudg-
led *T*, iugled *A.*   660 And] *blank in P.*   662 wife *P*] selfe
T-B.

Nowe in *Ioues* pallace that good lord doth supp
And drinke full bowles of *Nectar* in the skye.
Hunnies his page, that tasted of the cupp,
Did only lose his haire but did not dye.
True noble *Earle*, thy fame to heaven doth flye: 670
  He doth repent his fault and pardon craue,
  That mard thie bed and too soone made thie graue.

Thou didst behind thee leave a matchlesse sonne,
A peereles patterne for all princely *Peeres*,
Whose sparks of glorye in my tyme begunn,
Kindled with hope, flam'd highly in fewe yeeres,
But death him strooke, and drown'd his land with teeres.
  His sonne doth liue, true Image of him deade,
  To grace this soyle where showres of teares were shed.

The praise of Robt. Devoraux Late Earle of Essex

They were to blame that said the *Queene* should marry
With me her Horse-keeper—for soe they call'd me.
But thou, *Throgmorton*, which this tale didst carry
From *Fraunce* to *England*, hast more sharply gall'd me;
Sith my good *Queene* in Office high instal'd me,
  And I was Master of her highnesse horse,   685
  I scorne thie words which did my hate inforce.

The death of Sir Nicholas Throgmorton a verye worthie Knight

But tell me, Sir, how didst thou like the faire
When I to supper last did thee invyte?
If I did rid thee of a world of care
By giving the a Sallett, gentle Knight,
With gastly looks do not my soule affright.
  Lester I was, whome *England* once did dread,
  But nowe I am like thee, Throgmorton, dead.

Suspected to be poisoned with a sallett

690

668 *Hunnies* B] Hummnos *P*, Humings *T*, *etc.*   675 of my *P*.
681n, 682 Throgmorton] Frogmorton *P* (*recognized variant*).
685 hignesse *P*.

My Lord of *Sussex* was to chollericke,
That cal'd me Traytor and a Traytors sonne;
But I seru'd him a fine *Italian* tricke.
Had I not done soe, I had bin vndone.
Now marke the end: what conquest hath he wonn?
   A litle scruple that to him I sent
    Did purge his choller till his life was spent.

The death of the
moste noble
Earle of Sussex

700

He was a gallant Nobleman indeede.
O, but his life did still my life decrease.
Therefore I sent him with convenient speed
To rest amongst his ancestors in peace.
My rage was passified at his decease,
   And nowe I craue to embrace his love to late;
    Him dead I love, whome living I did hate.

705

I came to vissit, as I chanc'd to walke,
My Lady of *Lenox*, whome I found not well.
I tooke her by the hand, had priuate talke,
And soe departed, a shorte tale to tell.
When I was gon, into a flux she fell,
   That never ceas'd her companie to keepe
    Till it had brought her to a sencelesse sleepe.

The death of the
Countesse of Lenox

710

I dreampt she had not many daies to live,
And this my dreame did shortlie fall out true.
Soe as her ghostlie Father, I did giue
Some comforte to her Soule, for well I knewe
That she would shortly bid the world adiewe.
   Some say I gave such phisicke as did spill her,
    But I conceaue that meere conceite did kill her.

715

720

698 thend *P.*   702 increase *P.*   712 flax *P.*

[*32*]

Some will perhapps obiect I did pretend
To meete the *Earle of Ormond* on a daye
In single fight, our quarrell soe to end,
But did commaund my servant Killigray
To lie in Ambush, that stoute Lord to slaye.
    But heaven did not consent to worke his spoile,
    That was the glory of the Irishe soyle.

The death of the
Earle of Ormond
intended but not
effected
725

Perhapps I doubted that I was to weake,
And loath I was he should the conquest wynne.
If in this case I did my promise breake,
I hope men will not counpt yt for a synn.
Is yt not good to sleepe in a whole skynn?
    Where *Hanniball* could not prevaile by Blowes,
    He oft vs'd *Stratagems* to kill his foes.

730

735

Yf I the death of *Mounsieur Simiers* sought,
When he from *Fraunce* Ambassadour was sent,
I had iust cause to seeke yt, as I thought,
For towards me he bore noe good entente.
Had he not fled betimes, perhapps I ment
    To have sent him in Ambassage for my pleasure
    To the black *Kinge* that keeps *Auernus* treasure.

The death of
Mounsieure
Simiers Ambassa-
dour of the French
Kinge plotted but
not executed

For when noe man aboute the Court durst speake
That I had Ladie *Lettice* married,
This pratling frenchman first the Ice did breake
And to the *Queene* the fact discouered,
Which not without iust cause my anger bred:
    Thus the *Ape* did play his part, controld of none,
    When he espied the *Beare* from home was gone.

745

731 case *PX*] cause *TAB*.   736 *Simiers B*] *Sinniers P* (&
736n), *Sinuiers T, Symier X, Simers A*.   746 discoured *P*.

One *Saluatore*, an Italian borne,
Haveing once watch'd with me till midst of night,
Was found slaine in his bed the next daye morne.
Alas, poore man, I rue his woefull plight
That did in nothing but in synne delight:
   Had he to honest Actions bent his witt,   755
   He might have longer liu'd and scap't this fitt.

The death of an
Italian called
Saluatore

But what reward should such a man expect,
Whome Gold to anie lewdnes could entice?
Our turne once seru'd, why should not we reiect
Soe vile an Instrument of Damned vice?   760
What if he were dispatched in a trice?
   Was yt not better this mans bloud to spill
   Then lett him live, the world with sinne to fill?

Fallere Fallentem
non est fraus

I doubted least that *Doubty* would bewray
My counsell and with others partie take.   765
Wherefore, the sooner him to ryd awaye,
I sent him forth to *Sea* with Captaine *Drake*,
Who knewe how to entertaine him for my sake:
   Before he went, by me his lott was cast;
   His death was plotted and perform'd in hast.   770

He hoped well, but I did soe dispose
That he at *Port Sainct Gillian* lost his head,
Having noe tyme permitted to disclose
The inward greifs that in his mynd were bred.
We nothing feare the byting of the dead!   775
   Now lett him goe, transported by the Seas,
   And tell my secretts to th' Antipodes.

750 a *P.*   754 Thad *P.*   757n frauus *P.*   759 retect *P.*
764 *Doubty P (pun)*] *Doughty T-B.*   769 his *T-B*] this *P.*

My seruant *Gates* did speed as ill or worse,
To whome I did ,my close intents impart
And at his neede, with mony stuft his purse
And will'd him still take curradge to his harte.
Yet in the end he felt the deadly smarte:
He was inveagled by some subtill witted
To robb, soe he was taken and commytted.

The death of Gates
seruant to the
Earle of Lecester

Of pardon I did put him still in hope
When he of fellony was guiltie found,
And soe condemn'd, till his last freind, the rope,
Did him vphold from falling to the ground.
What hope of grace where vice doth soe abound?
He was beguild like Birds that vs'd to gape
At *Zeuxes* table for a painted grape.

785

790

Yet I did to the man noe iniurye:
I gaue him tyme and leasure to repent,
And well he knewe he had deseru'd to die.
Therefore, all future mischeife to preuent,
I let him slipp away with my consent:
For his repriuall, like a crafty fox,
I sent noe pardon, but an emptie box.

795

Els as vnfaithfull *Bannaster* betray'd
The *Duke of Buckingham*, his Master dere,
When he, of *Richards* tyrany affrayd,
Fled to his seruants house for succor there,
Soe might my man, for gaine or forc'd by feare,
Haue brought my corps with shame vnto the graue
By too much trusting of a paltry knave.

The falshood of
seruants to be
doubted

805

782 thend *P.*   801 affray'd *P.*

Meeseemes at me greate *Norfolks Duke* doth frowne
Because he thinks I did his death contriue,
Perswading some he aymed at the *Crowne*
And that by Royall match he ment to striue
A kingdome to his Lordshipp to deriue.   810
    Alas, good *Duke*, he was to meeke and mild,
    And I too faithlesse that his trust beguild.

The death of the
good Duke of
Norfolke

For when I found his humor first was bent
To take the Scotts captiud *Queene* to wife,
I egged him on to followe his intent,   815
That by this meanes I might abridg his life.
And shee, a crownlesse Queene, to stint all strife,
    First finding Scotland lost, to *England* fled,
    Where she, in hope of succor, lost her head.

The subtiltie of the
Earle of Lecester

O blessed spirits, liue ye evermore   820
In heavenly *Syon*, where your maker raignes,
And giue me leave my fortunes to deplore,
That am fast fettered with sinns Iron chaines.
Mans moste sweete ioyes are mixt with some sower
      paines,
    And none doth liue of high or low degree,   825
    In life or death that can from woe be free.

Ah, nowe my tongue growes werye to recite
Such massakers as haue bin heere exprest,
Whose sad remembraunce doth afflict my sprite.
Methinks I see legions of Saints to rest   830
In *Abrahams* bosome, and myselfe opprest:
    The burden of my Sinnes doe waie me downe;
    At me the fiends doe laugh and Angells frowne.

823 sinns. *P.*   825 now *P.*   829 sprite *as in* 362] spirit *PT.*

My crymes I graunt were greate and manifold,
Yet not soe hainous as some make reporte;   835
But flattering *Parrasits* are growne soe bold
That they of *Princes* matters make a sporte
To please the humors of the vulgar sorte,
    And that poore peeuish giddy headed crew
    Are prone to credit any tale vntrue.   840

Let those that live indeavor to live well,
Least after death theire guilt, like myne, remaine.
Let noe man thinke there is noe heaven nor hell,
Or with the impious Saduces mayntaine
That after death noe flesh shall rise againe.   845
    Let noe man trust in fickle fortunes wheele;
    The guerdon due for sinne in part I feele.

Knowe that the *Prince* of heavenly *Seraphins*,   Meaninge Lecester
When he gainst his creator did rebell,
Was tumbled downe for his presumptious sinnes;   850
Sathan (that once was blest) like lightening fell
From the highest heaven even to the depth of hell,
    And all those Angells that his part did take
    Haue nowe theire portion in the burning lake.

Of mightie heapes of Treasure I could vaunt,   The Earle of Leces-
For I reapt profitt out of every thinge.   ters meanes to gett
I could the *Prince* and peoples harts inchaunt   infinite Riches
With my faire words and smooth fac'd flattering.
Even out of drosse pure gold I oft did wringe,
    For though the meanes to gaine be oft vnmeete,   Bonus odor Luchri
    The smell of Lucre ever sauors sweete.   ex re qualibet

859 ought *P*, ought *corrected to* oft T.   860n requalibet *P*.

Soe sometimes I had singuler good happ By suits to the Queene
Greate suits of my dread Soueraigne to obteine.
Prodigall fortune powr'd downe from her lapp
Angells of gold as thicke as droppes of raine.   865
Such was my luck to find this golden vaine;
    Likewise to me yt seemed nothing strange By Changinge rents and lands with the Queene
    Both rents and lands oft with my prince to change.

I had another waye to enrich myself By Liscences
By getting Liscences for me alone   870
For Wyne, Oyle, Velluett, cloth, and such like pelfe,
By License, to, of Alienation,
By raiseing rents and by oppression,
    By clayming Forests, Pastures, Comons, Woods,
    And forfeiture of lands, of liues, and goods.   875

By this strange course alsoe I greatlie thriv'd, By fallinge out with the Queene
In falling out with my deare Soveraigne,
For I the plott soe cuningly contriu'd
That reconcilement soone was made againe,
And by this meanes great guifts I did obteine,   880
    For, that I might my baggs the better fill,
    I beg'd great suits as pledg of new good will.

Besids, I sometymes did encrease my store By placeinge of heades of houses in Oxford
By benefitt that I from *Oxford* tooke,
Electinge heads of houses heretofore:
I lou'd theire money and they lou'd theire booke.
Some poorer though more learned I forsooke,
    For in those daies your charitie wax'd cold—
    Litle was done for love, but much for gold.

867 seem'd *P*.   882 bag'd *P;* my good *P*.

Doubtlesse my Father was a valiaunt *Peere*
In *Edward* the sixths daies, when he was sent
Gainst rebells that did rise in *Northfolkshire*,
And after that when he to *Scotland* went
Vnder the *Lord Protectors* Regiment:
  By notable exploits against the Scott,
  Eternall glorie to himselfe he gott.

The vallour of the Earle of Warrwicke afterward Duke of Northumberland at Muscleborough feild & against the Rebells in Northfolke

Sureley Ambition was his greatest fault,
Which commonly in noble harts is bred,
He thought he neuer could his state exalt,
Till the good *Duke of Sommerset* was dead,
Who by my fathers meanes did loose his head,
  So ill the race of *Dudleys* could endure
  The *Seymours* liues, that did their fame obscure.

His ambition

The death of the Duke of Somersett

When once Kinge *Edward* att the butts had shott,
My *Father* sayd, your *Grace* shoots neare the white,
The King replied, but not so neare (I wott)
As when you shott my vncles head of quite,
The Duke my father knew the King spake right,
  And that he meant this matter to debate,
  If once he liud to come to mans estate.

The speech of the Earle of Northumberland to Edward the 6. and the Kings answere

910

It seemes my father in tymes past had beene
A skillfull *Archer*, though noe learned *Clarke*,
Soe strainge a chance as this is seldome seene,
I doe suppose he shott not in the darke,
That could soe quickly hitt soe faire a marke,
  Nor haue I mist my ayme, nor worse haue spedd
  When I shott of the *Duke of Norfocks* head.

915

897 *MS. R resumes (text and punctuation).*   897 *Sureley* R]
Truely *P-B.*   903 obscure *R.*

Tarquin the proud hearein we counted wise,
That he strooke of the highest poppies topp,
To note vnto his sonne, as I surmize,   920
That he the heads of some great peares should crop
Least they in time to high might chance to hopp:
   Excuse vs then, in that wee gaue such blowes,
   As chopt of heads of our aspiringe foes.

Now when the Duke of Somerset was dead,   The Duke of
My father to the *French* did *Bulloigne* sell.   Northumberland
As pleased him, the Kinge he governed,   sould Bolloigne to
And from the privie Councell did expell   the Frenchmen
Th' *Earles of South-Hampton*, and *of Arundell*,
   Thus whilst he ruled and controuled all,   930
   The wise yonge Kinge extreamly sick did fall;

Who having languisht long, of life deprived,   The death of King
Not without poyson, as it was suspected,   Edward the sixth
The *Councell* through my fathers meanes contriud,
That Suffocks daughter should be *Queene* elected;   935
The Sisters of Kinge *Edward* were reiected,
   My Brother *Gilford* to *Iane Gray* was wedded,
   To high preferd, to be so soone beheaded.

This *Lady Iane*, that once was tearmd a *Queene*,   The Lady Iane a
Greater in fame, then fortune was putt downe,   vertuous Dame
Had not Kinge *Henryes Daughters* livinge beene,   proclaymed
Might for her vertues haue deserud a *Crowne*,   Queene and shortly
Fortune one her at once did smyle and frowne: after beheaded
   Her wedding garment for a Princesse meet,
   Was quickly changed for a windinge-sheete.   945

922 hopp *R.*   926 sell *R.*   928 expell *RX*] depell *PTAB.*
931 fall *R.*   943 *missing in R, text of T (punct. editorial).*
945 -sheete *R.*

Betweene the *Duke of Suffocke*, and my father,
The match was made, which *Death* soone after brake,
But by my fathers subtle drifts I gather,
He meant *Queen Marie* his owne wife to make,
If it had binne his fortune her to take,
    And then to make the former purpose voyde,
    The race of *Suffocke* should haue bin destroyd.

My Father was by his familiar tould,
He by a man should neuer be subdude,
Whereon he grew more peremptorie bould,
The issue of King *Henrie* to exclude
From Kingdoms sway: the sprite did him delude,
    For when King *Edward* that good Prince was dead,
    A *Woeman* Raignd, that made him loose his head.

He with a warrant from the Councells hands,
His dayes sett downe and iorneys limited,
Most bravely furnisht with his martiall bands
Rode t' apprehend *Dame Marie*, who for dread,
And dainger of her life to *Norfocke* fledd,
    But whilst from *London* he abroad did rainge,
    Mens minds did alter, as the times did chainge.

For Princesse Marie was by *Trumpets* sound,
Proclaimed *Queen*, and in the *Throne* invested,
And he at *Cambridge* beeing quickly found,
Was of high *Treazon* instantly arrested,
By those at whome he lately scoft, and iested,
    Soe to the *Tower* he being once convayd,
    His head not longe vppon his shoulders stayd.

950

955

960

965

The Duke of
Northumberlands
intent to marrye
Queene Marye

She is proclaim'd
Queene The Duke
of Northumber-
land arrested of
high treason att
Cambridge

His death

952 destroyd *R.*   957 delude *R.*   958 dead *R.*   959
head *R.*   973 stayd *R.*

Like th' Apples which *Gomorrhas Trees* doe beare,
Whose Towne with fire and brimstone was combust,   975
Of cullor like to gold, they yet appeare,
Or like the fruict that tempted *Eue* to lust,
But being tutcht, foorthwith they turne to dust,
   And though they seeme soe beautifull to sight,
    They yeald noe sapp that may the tast delight.   980

Soe seems a *Crowne* to an Ambitious wight
Most rutilant, and splendent in aspect
That doth with glittringe showes beguile the sight,
And doth corrupt the inward Intellect
With superficiall beauties fond respect,   985
   And if by wrongfull meanes it be obteynd,
    Nothing but care, distruste and feare is gaind.

I did but like weake *Icarus* assay
After my sire Northumberland to flye
With wexen wings, which soone will melt away,   990
My plumes were like the wings of *Mercurie*,
When he coms in embassage from the skie,
   By wisedome, wealth, by warinesse, and witt,
    I fled aloft and there did safely sitt.

My haples *Grandfather* did loose his head,   995
Who for his private gaine abusde the state,
My father after him as badly sped,
Havinge incurd the Prince and peoples hate.
My courage for their fall did not abate,
   But growne more warie by their dismal haps,   1000
    I learned how to prevent such afterclaps.

Terminal punctuation supplied at 974, 975, 979 (-t, *frayed*),
980, 987, 995, 998, 1000, 1001.

As *Richard Duke of Yorke* when through submission,
And iust desert into the lapse he fell,
And being likewise held in great suspition,
As one that oft attempted to rebell,   1005
To th' end thenceforth he might more safely dwell,
Did soe provide after the former breach,
To come noe more within his princes reache.

Soe I knowinge my fault, made my selfe stronge,
By force, by faction, and by flatterye,
By guifts, by threats, by my enchanting tongue,
By fraud, by frendship, by humilitie,
By sleights, and *Machavellian* policie,
That if I once deserud my Princes anger,
I might noe more be catcht within her dainger.   1015

Sith at a *Diademme* my thoughts did ayme,
And that I saw how things acrosse did goe,
When for myselfe the *Crowne* I could not claime,
Because thereto noe title I could shewe,
Then one my freind I would the same bestowe,   1020
About whose person I might beare most swaye,
As one borne to commaund, not to obay.

For I was iumpe of *Iulius Cæsars* mind,
That could noe one superior lord endure,
Nay, I to guid my soueraigne was enclind,   1025
And bringe the common people to my lure,
Accounting that my fortune was obscure,
And that I liued in a woefull plight,
If any one eclipst my glories light.

1003 fell *R.*   1025 Nay *R.*

The Lo: of Leces-
ters circumspect
dealinge

He aymeth at the
Crowne

〖*43*〗

The loue to raigne makes many men respect
Neither their frinds, their kindred nor their vowe;
The love to raigne makes many men neglect
The dutie which to god and man they owe,
From out this fountayne many mischeefs flow:
    Heareof examples many may be read,
    In *Cronicles* of th' English princes dead.

The Ambitious desire of principallitie and what it worketh

1035

This humor made *Kinge Harold* breake his oth,
Made vnto *William* Duke of Normandye,
This made king *Rufus*, and young *Beauclarke* both,
Their elder brother Robert to defie,
And *Stephen* to forgett his loyaltie
    To *Maud* the Empresse, and to hold in scorne
    The faithfull Oath that he to her had sworne.

Kings which broake theire othes to obtaine the Kingdome Henry surnamed Beauclarke for his learninge

This made yonge *Henrie* crowned by his *Syre*
Against his father warr-fare to mainteyne,
This made King *Iohn* the Kingdom to aspire
Which to his *Nephewe Arthur* did perteyne,
And him in prison hardly to detayne,
    And this made Bullingbrooke t' usurpe the *Crowne*,
    Puttinge his lawfull *Souueraigne Richard* downe.

1045

1050

This made *Edward* the fowerth at his retourne
From *Burgundie*, when he to *Yorke* was come,
To breake the Oth which he had lately sworne,
And rule the Realme in good *King Henries* roome,
This made the *Tyrant Richard* eke to doome
    His *Nephews* death, and rid away his wief,
    And soe in blood to end his wretched life.

Edward the Fowrth

1055

1031 vowe *R.*   1034 flow *R.*   1054 *henries R.*

A *pretty plott* in practice I did putt,
Either to take a *Queene* without delaye,
Or when the cards were shuffled, and well cutt,   1060
To chuse a King and cast the Knaues away,
He should be cunninge, that great game will play,
   Ill lucke hath he that noe good game can make,
   When Princes play and crownes lie at the stake.

First I assaid *Queene Elsabeth* to wedd,   1065
Whome diuers princes courted but in vaine,
When in this course vnluckely I sped,
I sought the *Scotts Queens* marriage to obteyne,
But when I reapt noe profitt of my payne,
   I sought to match *Denbigh* my tender child   1070
   To *Dame Arbella*, but I was beguild.

Euen as *Octauius* with *Mark Anthonie*
And *Lepidus* the *Roman Empire* shard,
That of the World then held the *Souueraigntie*,
Soe I a newe Triumvirate prepard,   1075
If *Death* a while yonge *Denbies* life had spard,
   The Grandame, Vncle, and the Father in lawe,
   Might thus haue brought all England vnder awe.

But when I saw my witt had noe more might,
To gett a royall match then if I striud   1080
By washing oft, to make an *Æthiope* white,
And when I saw my sonne of life depriud,
Arbella lost, and I my hopes surviud,
   I plotted to advance vnto the *Crowne*
   One of my kinne, a Lord of good renowne.   1085

1064 stake *R*.   1074 then] the *R*.   1078 awe *R*.   1081
white *R*.

[45]

Soe I preferd *Hastings* before those other,
Which from th' vnited royall blood descende,
Although he came but of a second brother
Of Yorks right heyre, alone I did pretend
His claime was iust, and this I would defend,   1090
   Yet I did know his title was to weake
   And might haue donne more harme than I will speak.

For if Yorks title were advanc'd againe
Lankaster also would his clayme recall,
In whose defence were many thousands slayne,   1095
Now the remainder of this howse doth fall
To th' *heyres of Castile*, and of *Portagalle*,   A weake title.
   And soe should right of consequence pertayne
   To *Her* that is th' *Infanta* now of Spaine.

Braue Iohn of *Gaunt*, *Edward* the thirds fowrth sonne,   Iohn of Gaunt, and
Had two Sonns, *Henrie* that was after Kinge,   his issue.
Whoe brought the *Crowne* to *Lankaster*, and Iohn,
From whome Henry the Seauenth his claime did bringe,
And Daughters twayne, by *Blanche*, and *Constance*
    spring,
   Phillip, Iohn Kinge of Portugal did wed,   1105
   And *Katterne* th' *Heyre* of Castile married.

Yet noe one part can mearely clayme the *Crowne*,
But such as from both howses are deriud,
The heavens vppon this Lande did euer frowne,
While *Yorke* and *Lankaster* togeather striud,   1110
The case seemd doubtfull till it was contriud,
   That *Richmond* matching with *Fowerth Edwards*
    daughter,
   Both should posses the crowne, and end all slaughter.

Punctuation supplied in 1089, 1092, 1093, 1094, 1100, 1103,
1111, 1112.   1098 consequenc *R.*   1103 henry *R.*   1110
Wile *R.*

For neither *Marius* and proud *Syllas* wares,
In *Rome* such bloody massakers did breede,   1115
Nor *Cæsar*, and great *Pompeys* ciuill iares,
Nor *Guelfes*, and *Ghibilines* did cause to bleed
Soe many harts, though longe they disagreede,
As *Yorke*, and *Lankaster*, whose mortall hate
Consumd themselues, and halfe vndid the state.   1120

It were to tedious for me to receite
Howe many *Princes* of the *Royall* blood,
Were done to death by treason or in fight,
In what vncertaine state this Kingdome stoode,
What brainsick lightnes, and what furious moode   1125
  Possest the Commons, that would haue the Crowne
  Euen like a foote-balle tossed vp and downe.

King Edward the thirds sonne this strife did breed
But the first cause that did their hate inflame,
From Henrie the thirds Children did proceede,   1130
Edward, and Edmond Crookback, from whome came
In fowerth decent a Daughter, *Blanch* by name,
  She married Iohn of Gaunt whose son and heire
  Calld Bullingbrooke possest the regall chaire.

Richard of Burdeux was the eldest sonne   1135
To Edward Prince of Wales, the blacke Prince hight,
Sonne to Third Edward, soe the strife begune,
When *Henrie Duke of Lankaster* by might
Compeld *Kinge Richard* to resigne his right
  Vnto himselfe, although the title fell   1140
  To him that matcht with th' *hayre of Lionell*.

1120 state *R.*   1126 th Crowne *R.*   1130 Childredn *R.*
1135 burdeux *R.*

Soe when the *Crowne* had three descents remaynd
Vnder the rule of th' House of *Lankaster*,
Then Edward duke of Yorke the Crowne obtaynd
By *Phillip* wife of Edmond Mortimer,   1145
Lyonels hayre, who did the right transferre
  To *Anne*, espousd to *Duke Plantagenet*,
    At *Wakefield* slayne, whose son the *Crowne* did gett.

Some saye that Edmund Crooke-backe (from whose line
Old Iohn of Gaunt deriud his petegree)   1150
Was Longshankes elder brother, and in fine
Put by the crowne for his deformitie,
If this be true, I doe noe reason see
  But that in my conceit I should preferre
    Before Yorks race, the Howse of *Lankaster*.   1155

If this be false, Yorke is of greater fame,
And worthy to possesse the royall chaire,
Although this from Third Edwards Fift son came,
For that it cupled in coniunction faire
With *Lionel* the *Duke of Clarence Heyre*,   1160
  Which Duke (if wee vnto the truth will graunt)
    Was elder brother vnto Iohn of Gaunt.

Henry of Monmouth with small paine, and cost,
Did conquere France but he not longe did raigne,
Henrie of Windsor long time liu'd but lost   1165
All that his sire, or Grandsire did obteine,
And soe died in the Tower; his sonne was slayne
  At *Teuxburie*, the Battayle being ended,
    And soe the Crowne to Yorke more firme descended.

Terminal punctuation supplied at 1147, 1148, 1169; *internal at*
1153, 1156, 1167.   1160 *of Om. R.*   1165 Winsor *R.*

Fowrth Edward had two sonns and daughters five,   1170
Both princly sonns were murd'red in the *Tower*,
Richard the last heyre male of Yorke aliue,
Was slaine at Bosworth field by *Richmonds* power,
Whoe matcht with Edwards heire, Yorkes fayrest flower,
   Three yonger daughters meanly were bestowd,   1175
   The last a *Nunne*, Religious life she vowde.

Perceaving that the dainger was soe great,
For one to giue a Kingdom to his frende,
I would haue rather kept the Kingly seate,
Than giuen it any one, that in the end,   1180
Might proue vnthankfull and perhaps intend,
   If once the *Crowne* were setled on his head,
   To *cracke* my crowne, till I to death had bled.

When any mans true love I meant to trie,
His meaning by this *Watch-woord* I did knowe,   1185
What, are you setled? if he did replie
In doubtfull tearmes, or this poore answer, (noe,)
He was not for my turne, I lett him goe,
   But if he answeard, setled is my hart,
   O, him I held, a man of high desart.   1190

Sith I could doe myselfe but little good,
Vnlesse I kindled strife among the Peares,
Or sett the Princes of the royall bloode,
Amonge themselues togeather by the eares,
Or fild the Commons harts with doubtfull feares,   1195
   Marke what a subtle plott I did devise,
   To compasse that which gaue me meanes to rise.

1170 daughter *R.*   1175 bestowd *R.*

First Huntingtonn should Scottlands Kinge defeate;
Arbella, Huntington. The *Queene*, in ward,
Should putt them downe, and challenge *Cynthias* seate,   1200
Yet she reserud aliue, for my stronge guard;
If fortune one my part had fallen out hard,
   I might haue vsd th' authoritie of all,
   To mount the *Throne*, and trivmph at their fall.

The *Beare* was ready euermore to watch   1205
That the *Red Lion* might be soone supprest,
That the Black Bull or Wolfe smalle vantage catch,
That the *Sole Bird*, that hath the flaminge crest,
Should in *Arabia* build noe stately nest,
   And that fayre Foule, that doth Ioues lightninge
     beare,   1210
   His clipped wings, but hardly should vpreare.

Loe thus the *Beare* still loved to controule,
Since *Archas* and *Calisto* were enstald,
In the *Celestiall* Globe, neare th' *Artict Pole*,
Which now the great, and lesser *Beares* are cald,   1215
Soe I that to Ambition was enthrald,
   Desird to climbe, and I ascended high,
   But often fayled when I meant to flie.

I tooke such order that noe man should blaze
The Name of him that should the *Queene* succeede.   1220
Thus did I put the Commons in a maze
And made them feare, more then was cause indeede,
That *Cynthias* Death, would make all England bleede.
   All men might guesse, but none directly saye,
   This is the *Heyre* that shall this Kingdome swaye.   1225

Terminal punctuation supplied at 1198, 1201, 1204, 1207, 1210,
1218, 1220, 1223.   1199 *Arbella* Huntington, the *Queene R.*
1217 Desire *R.*

When *Richard Cœur-de-Lyon* did prepare
To take his voyage for the *Holy Land*,
Arthur of Brittayne was proclaymed hayre,
In solemne manner by the Kings comaund:
When *Second Richard* with his martiall band   1230
  To *Ireland* sayld, he likewise did preferre,
  As his next *Heire, Sir Edmund Mortimer.*

But I procurd an Act of Parlament,
Willinge the *Heyre* apparant to conceale,
A strange device and fitt for their intent   1235
That seeke the *Crowne*, by meare deceit to steale,
But most pernicious to the Publique Weale,
  Saue that Gods providence doth so dispose
  That *Right* takes place, though it hath many foes.

Although this new-found statute bore pretence   1240
Of safegard to the *Queene*, if throughly weighed,
It might haue bred great danger and offence,
Which gaue vs leave our friends closely to ayde,
And made the simpler sort of men affrayd,
  T' enquire thereof, for feare t' offend the Lawe,   1245
  Whilst on our side great numbers we might draw.

For vnder cullor therby to restrayne,
Some that would seeke t' eclipse fayre *Cynthias* light,
We priuilie did harbor, and mainteyne
A route of ruffins, quickly armd to fight   1250
In the defence of some vnworthy wight
  Whome wee might haue sett vp within an hower,
  To daunt the *Queen*, or true successors power.

1237 Weale *R.*   1238 did *R.*   1246 draw *R.*

Yet in excuse, this parable I tould,
Men honor more the Sun when it doth rise,   1255
Than when it Setts; so when the *Queen* waxt old,
And th' heyre made knowne, growes popular, and wise,
His sight might draw the Peoples harts, and eyes,
  To waite on him, whose thoughts were fixt before
  Vppon th' old Prince whome they did all adore.   1260

Some hop't to lade their backes with others spoyles,
Others did feare supposd *Corriuals* strife,
Forraigne invasion, and intestine broyles,
Woe to the Husband, mourninge to the wief,
Some wisht the world would end with *Cynthias* life.   1265
  Others did feare least that in time to come
  Young babes should liue to weepe on *Cynthias* toombe.

But now Kinge Ieames, the *Monarch* of this soyle,
Inaugurate by Heauen and Earthes consent,
Like *Salomon*, annoynted with the oyle   1270
Of gladnes, and of grace, from Scone is sent,
To be *Great Brittaines* greatest Ornament,
  And to establish newe the golden Age,
  In spite of *Spite*, and maugre *Envies* rage.

Thus having tould a *Catalogue* of crimes,   1275
Which to my charge haue publikely binne layd,
With some excuse, how I observed tymes,
To rayse my state, how mightilie I swayd,
Whilst I within this kingdoms limitts staied,
  Now will I shewe, what Fame I gott or lost,   1280
  Whilst I did frolicke on the *Belgic* coast.

Final punctuation supplied at 1257, 1261, 1265, 1281.   1258
eys, *R.*   1259 before, *R.*   1268 Ieames *R.*   1273 th *R.*

In the *Lowe Countries* did my Fame soare high,
When I was sent Liuetenant-generall,
The *Queens* proud foes I stoutlie did defie
And made them to some composition falle,
There I mayntaind a port maiesticall,
  In pompe and trivmph many daies I spent,
  From *Noble*, then my name grew *Excelent*.

The Earle of
Lecesters voyage
into the lowe
Countryes
1285

Then was my hart in heighth of his desire,
My mind puft vp with surquedrie, and pride,
The vulgar sort my glorie did admire,
Euen as the *Romans*, *Aue Cæsar*, cride,
When th' Emperor to the *Senate* howse did ride,
  Soe did the *Flemings* with due reverence,
  Like *Thunder* speake, God saue your Excellence!

1290

His excellencye

Fewe Subiects before me obteynd this stile
Vnlesse they were as viceroyes of the Land,
The name of Lordship seemd to base and vile,
To me that gouernd such a royall bande,
And had a Princes absolute commaunde.
  Who did not of my puissance stand in awe,
  That might put him to death by martiall Lawe?

1300

Loe what a Title hath mine honor gott,
An Excellencie added to my name,
Can this iniurious world soe quickly blott
A name soe great out of *Records of Fame?*
Couer my glory with a vayle of shame?
  Or will it now contemne me, being dead,
  Whom living, euen with feare it honored?

1305

1286 miesticall, *R.*   *Final punctuation supplied at* 1288,
1295, 1308.   1289 my *P-B*] *Om. R.*   1300 commaunde, *R.*
1308 me *R.*

The Towne cald *Dewsborough* I did beseige,
Which did on composition shortly yeald,
I did good service to my gratious Liege,
Till by ill Counsellours I was beguilde,
For such as were my captaines in the Field,
   To whome at length cheefe charge I did committ,
   Seduc'd me to doe many things vnfitt.

When Sir Iohn Norris councell I refusde,
Whose perfect skill in feats of Arms I knew,
By Rowland York's aduice I was abusd,
Whereon some losse soone after did ensewe,
Deuenter Towne and *Zutphen* Sconce, I rewe,
   By *Yorke*, and *Stanly* without any blowes,
   Were rendred to the mercie of the foes.

And that which to my hart more greif might strike,
Hapned the Death of that redoubted Knight,
My *Nephew Sydney*, who neare Colestone Dike,
Receaud his deadly wound, through Fortunes spite,
I sent noe fresh supplie to him in fight,
   I was not farre of, with a mighty hoast,
   Soe with his losse of life, some fame I lost.

The *Court* in him lost a brave *Courtier*,
The *Country* lost a guide, theire faults to mende,
The *Campe* did loose an expert *Souldier*,
The *Cittie* lost an honorable frende,
The *Schooles* a *Patrone*, their right to defend,
   The *Court*, the *Country*, the *Camp*, *Schooles*, and *Cittie*,
   For *Sydnies* death still singe a dolefull dittie.

The towne of
Deusborough
taken by the Lo:
of Lecester vpon
Composition

1315

Deuenter towne
and Zutphen
Sconce by Sir
Rowland Yorke
and Captaine
Stanley yeelded vp
to the enimyes

The death of Sir
Phillipp Sidney

1330

1335

Final punctuation supplied at 1315, 1318, 1319, 1325, 1330,
1332, 1334, 1337.   1317n Zulphen [*blank*] *P* (*which misreads
soone* 1321).   1319 Rowlands *R; aduice R*] deuice *P-B*.
1322 any *R*] manie *P-B*.   1325 redoubted *RT*] renowned
PXAB.   1326 *Syney R*.

Now while my Princly glory did abound,
Like ritch *Lucullus* I great feasts did make,
And was for hospitalitie renownd,
The vse of Armes I quickly did forsake,
An easier taske I meant to vndertake,
  I tooke no Ioy in wounds, or broken pates,
  But to carouse and banquet with the States.

The Earle of
Lecesters Hospital-
itie and feastings
in the lowe
Countries

Not *Heliogabalus*, whose dainty fare,
Did all the *Roman Emp'rours* feastes exceede
In cost, and rarenes might with mine compare,
Though he on braynes of *Ostrages* did feede
And *Phœnicopteries*, and that insteede
  Of Oyle, he vsd with *Balme* his lamps to fill,
  Such was the pleasure of this *Tyrants* will.

1345

Phœnicopterus a
byrd of whome
Plinie writeth that
hath Crimson
wings

To me *Count Egmonds* daughters did resort,
And such braue Dames as Flanders then did yeald,
That it did seeme I rather came to court
A gallant Ladie, then to pitch a fielde,
For I did lay aside the sword and shield,
  At cards and dice I spent the vacant dayes,
  And made great feasts insteede of martiall frayes.

The Countesse of
Egmonds daugh-
ters resorteinge to
my Lo: of Lecester

1355

But while in games, and love my tyme I spent,
Seeminge secure as if I carde for nought,
My messengers abroad I daylie sent,
As instruments of my still woorkinge thought,
Whereby my purpose oft to passe I brought,
  And compast what I did before devise,
  At such a time as noe man would surmise.

1360

1365

1349 insteede, *R.*   1350 fill *R.*   1352 daughters *RX*]
Daughter *PTAB* (*see notes*).

Thus great attempts I oft did enterprize,
Like a *Magician* that with some fine wile,
Dazels the sight of the *Spectators* eyes,
And with illusions doth their sence beguile,
Such policies my cunninge did compile,
    That I before mens eyes did cast a mist,
    While I performd such matters as I list.

His pollicye when he was at his pastymes

1370

Ye that like *Apes* doe imitate my deeds,
Hopeing thereby like favor to obteyne,
Know that soe high a spirite neuer breeds,
In a blunt pesant or vnnurturd swayne,
But in my hart imperious thoughts did raigne,
    Noe flegmatick dull milk-sopp can aspire,
    But one compact of th' Element of fier.

His Councell to younge Courtiers

1375

He dayly must devise some stratagem,
He must be ritch, stout, liberall, and wise,
The humors of base men he must contemne,
He must be gratious in the peoples eyes,
He should be furnisht with rare qualities,
    With learning, iudgment, policie, and witt,
    And such like parts, as for the Courte are fitt.

The Complements of a right Courtier

1385

For every forward fellow is not borne,
To be a *Scipio*, or a *Maximus*,
Vnlesse that wisdome doth his state adorne
Or valure make his life more glorious,
Though he be base of byrth like *Marius*,
    Yet he by vertues ayd, aloft maye come,
    Like him that seaven tymes Consul was in Rome.

1390

Marius a poore mans sonne was chosen 7 times Consull in Rome

1371 eys *R.*   *Final punctuation supplied at* 1372, 1378, 1380,
1386, 1393.   1380 some *P-B*] *Om. R.*   1386 parets *R.*

Ventidius Name at first was meane and base,
Till he the *Parthians* hoast had ouerthrowne,
And *Cicero* came of ignoble race,
Borne at *Arpinum*, a poore Country towne,
Yet he made Arms giue place vnto the Gowne,
   And *Rome* by his great wisedome freed from spoyle
   Calld him the Father of his natiue soyle.

Ventidius quid
enim Quid Tullius
anne aliud quam
sidus et occulti
miranda potentiali
celi—Iuvenall:

1400

Perhaps younge *Courtiers* sometime learne to singe,
To scipp or dance before their mistris face,
To tutch like *Orpheus*, some enchanting stringe,
To runne at tilte, to iett with stately pace,
Or by some fine discourse to purchase grace,
   But cannott mannage the affayres of state
   Which best belongs to each great Potentate.

1405

Listen to me, ye lusty *Cauiliers*,
That in high favor doe attempt to grow,
Experience bred in me these many yeares,
Hath taught me cunninge which ye doe not know:
Some precepts heare I doe intend to shew
   And if my *Syren-Songe* please not great Peeres,
   Then may they with *Vlisses* stopp their eares.

1410

Trust not a frind that is new reconcild—
In loues fayre shew he may hide fowle deceite.
By him ye vnawares may be beguild.
Reaveale to none your matters of great weight,
If aney chance to knowe your lewde conceite,
   Suspected to bewray your bad intent,
   He ought to suffer death or banishment.

Trust not a recon-
ciled freind

1420

Final punctuation supplied at 1398, 1400, 1401, 1407, 1411,
1415, 1416, 1417.   1408 me *R; Cauiliers R*] Souldiers *P-B*.
1414 Then may they *X-B*] That may *R*, They may *PT*.

Caligula the *Scourge* of famous *Rome*
Wisht all the *Romans* had one only head,
That when he list to giue their fatall doome,
He might with one great blowe stricke all them dead,
Soe should he neuer neede their hate to dread,
   Euen such a mischeefe wisht I to my foes—
    That many men might perish with fewe blowes.

The Emperor
Caligula wisht all
the Romans had
but one heade that
he might strike
them all of att
one blowe.

But vnto those that doe your favor seeke,
And by your helpe, hope their lowe states to rayse,
Ye must be curteous, bountefull, and meeke,
Cæsar by *Clemencie* woone greatest prayse,
And was esteemd the *Miror* in his dayes,
   For it belongs to men of great estate,
    To spare the poore, and ritch mens pride t' abate.

1430

Cæsar the Mirror
of Clemency

1435

Its ill to be a rubb vppon the ground,
Wherein the Prince the allie minds to sweepe,
Their owne estates they fondly doe confound
That into high attempts soe boldly creepe,
And with their shallow pates doe wade soe deepe,
   To hinder what their *Soueraigne* doth intend,
    Or to controll what they cannot amende.

Noli altum sapere

Its dangerous to
rowse the Lyon
when he is asleepe

Callisthenes muche torment did susteyne,
Because great *Alexanders* pride he checkt.
Graue *Seneca* (choosinge his *Death*) was slayne
By *Neroes* doome, whose faults he did correct;
Vse not to sharpe rebukes but haue respect
   Vnto the Persons; when great men do euill,
    The vengeaunce leaue to god, or to the Diuell.

1445

Final punctuation supplied at 1427, 1444, 1448, 1449.   1447
to *P-B*] *Om. R.*

Be not to haughty, pride procureth hate,
And meane mens hate may turne to your disgrace,
Nor be ye to familier in high state,
For that will breede contempt amonge the base,
Obserue a mean which winneth noe meane grace,
    Speake faire to all, trust fewe, vse well your foes,
    For this may purchase love, where hatred growes.

A meeke and modest carriadge required

1455

If ye doe feare least that your freind should chance,
To mount to highly in the *Princes* grace,
His prayse to heaven, then sticke not to advance,
Say that the charge he beareth is too base,
And that his woorth deserues farre better place,
    Soe may ye by this praise rid him awaye,
    And soe supplye his place another daye.

A waye to procure ones ouerthrowe by praisinge him

1460

Say he will proue a *Terror* in the fielde,
This priuate life doth much obscure his fame,
More fitt to beare great *Aiax* seaven-fold shield,
Than like *Sardanapale*, to court a Dame.
He idlely liues at home, it is a shame,
    Her verie presence may his foes appalle,
    Let him be sent *Liuetenaunt Generall.*

If he be valliant thus

1470

Now if he chance to perishe in some fighte,
It was not your woorke but the chance of warrs,
Or thus you may excuse yourselues by slight,
Blaminge the Influence of the angrie Starrs
That thus by death his future fortune barrs,
    And sighinge, *wee are sorye,* ye may saye,
    That this braue man would cast himselfe awaye.

1475

1451 means *R.*   1455 fewe *RT*] none *PXAB.*   *Final
punctuation supplied at* 1456, 1467, 1472.   1460 carge *R.*
1463 *hi R.*

But if in feats of Armes he hath noe skill,

If he be learned and eloquent:

If he be learned, wise, or eloquent,
By praysing him thus may you worke your will: 1480
Procure him in Embassage to be sent,
Farre of, least he retourne incontinent,
    As to the mighty *Cham*, or Prester Iohn,
    And trivmph in his roome when he is gonne.

If ye would fayne cause him to be envide,   1485
Say that he beares a very royall minde,
The common people love him as their guide,
He is soe gratious, affable, and kinde,
In him some sparks of maiestie they finde,
    Thus may his prayse turne to his greevous smart,   1490
    And breede suspicion in the *Princes* hart.

It skills not mutch, if ye can paint or noe,
To sett fayre collours on your wooden Loue,
Although th' *Italian Courtier* taught ye soe,
This art let *Zeuxes*, or *Apelles* prove,   1495
Dead pictures did not my affections moue,
    Lett Painters drawe fayre *Venus* comely face,
    Noe shadowe, but the substance we embrace.

It boots not to excell in Musicks arte,
In prayse thereof, I list not to dispute,   1500
It better pleasd great *Alexanders* hart,
To see *Achilles* speare then *Paris* Lute,
Braue Alcibiades mislikt the Flute,
    And for my part sith Musicke ioyes the eare,
    I loud to heare it, but noe part to beare.   1505

Final punctuation supplied at 1480, 1487, 1505.   1490 sma *R*
(*margin frayed*).

It needs not to excell in *Poets* rimes,
To versifie is but a pretty toye,
Wherewith to passe away some idle times,
And make longe time seeme short with longing ioye,
While men doe prayse their Ladies faire, but coye,   1510
   Let Bards sit plodding on their learning layes,
   Whilest ye sitt plottinge deeds to win high prayse.

If ye doe *Princly* regiment affecte,
Ye must be mutch more humble then before,
Beare a high mind, but countenance deiect,   1515
Shewing a kinde of pittie to the poore,
Chiefly to such as doe your helpe implore.
   Sometyme conforme ye to the Peoples will,
   And sooth their humors, be they good, or ill.

When *Nero*, fierce *Domitian* and the rest   1520
Of wicked Emp'rours that in *Rome* did raigne
Permitted vice, the People loud them best,
Which when good *Pertinax* would needs restraine,
He in a mutenye was shortly slaine,
   Wherefor whoe can this argument convince: 1525
   He was a good Man, but a silly Prince.

Henrie the *Sixth* was holy and devout,
Who when his subiects fought, still fell to prayer,
Gentle in Peace, in battayle nothing stout,
Which gave occasion to the *Yorkish heyre*,   1530
To seate himselfe in *Henries* royall Chaire,
   Wherefore of him, in the like sort I sing,
   He was a good man, but a simple kinge.

Final punctuation supplied at 1517, 1523, 1525, 1526.   1527
dvout, *R.*   1529 battaye *R.*

But *Richard* the Vsurper, puttinge downe
His princly *Nephewes*, causd them to be slaine,   1535
Yet when he did possesse the regall *Crowne*,
Good Lawes he made, and Iustice did mainteyne,
And as a Righteous Prince a while did raigne,
    Wherefore denye this argument whoe can,
    He was a good *Kinge*, though an euill man.   1540

So *Mackbeth* that in Scotland sometime raignd
When first he had Kinge *Duncans* Death compact,
Yet when he had the *Garlande* once obteynd
Which he by force uniustly did detract,
Diuers good statutes then he did enacte,   1545
    And soe of him the former songe I singe,
    He was a bad man, but an honest Kinge.

Let not my words allure great men to vice,
But lett them take example by the best,
The sinns of wicked men ought to suffice   1550
That other men may learne them to detest,
And of all euills lett them chuse the lest,
    Want of discretion is noe little fault,
    In those whom God to honor doth exalte.

Many more subtell secrets I could tell,   1555
Saue that some captious people will suspecte,
I am to deeply seene in *Machauell*,
And the seuere *Criticall Stoicke* seckt,
That do presume mens manners to correct,
    Will censure ill of this my harmles speach,   1560
    Wherein true rules of policie I teach.

Punctuation supplied at 1539, 1542, 1545.   1550 suffice
emendation] be knowe *R* (*only text*).

Who soe would faine be thought an vpright man,
In State affayres to meddle let him shunne
In times corrupt, as Cato *Vtican*,
Did giue this rule in precept to his sonne,   1565
For he must needs into great hatred runne,
    Vnlesse with others he will serue the times,
    And be in sort copartner of their crimes.

Nowe to proceede in tellinge on the storie,
Of such attempts as I did enterprize,   1570
Whereby I hop'd to winne eternall glorye,
I dayly did contemplate and devise,
How I by Force, or policie might rise,
    To be a king, or such a kinglike Peare,
    As wanting but the name, cheefe sway might beare.   1575

Soe though I did in secret sort conspire,
For private gaine, against the publicke state,
Or seeke aboue my calling to aspire,
Stirr factions, taxe the commons, sett debate,
Or on the livings of poore men ingrate,   1580
    What I intended many might surmize,
    But noe man durst my name to scandalize.

For I had gott an act of Parlement,
That none gainst privie Councellors should prate,
But he should suffer condigne punishment,   1585
That vrg'd by envie, or malitious hate,
Would with a foolish toungue, and knauish pate
    Talke Idly of our persons that did deale,
    In weightey busines for the publike weale.

1575 name *R.*   1578 aboute *R.*   1589 weale *R.*

[*63*]

Thus did I bridle each mans lavish tongue,   1590
That in full cupps, yet with an empty witt,
Vomiting forth his malice, did vs wronge,
Misconstruing such decrees as wee thought fitt
Who gravely did at Councell table sitt,
    Discussing matters of noe little waight,   1595
    Aboue the reach of common mens conceyte.

Now I that was impatient of delayes,
Doubtinge least fitter tyme I should not finde
Than in the raigne of *Cynthias* happye dayes,
To compasse what I had conceaud in minde,   1600
Having the *Princes* power to me assignd,
    Vnto my vse their forces did employe,
    That what I would by force I might enioye.

For when the Campe at *Tilburie* did lie,
Some shrewdly did suspect that I was bent   1605
To ayd the Spanish hoast, if happilie,
They had arriud on th' English continent,
I lovd them not, though as an Instrument
    I might haue vsd them to bringe forces in,
    That to my selfe great honor I might winne.   1610

This was the Yeare from Christs nativitie,
A thousand, and fiue hundred, eighty eight,
Of which some men did strange things prophesie,
Euen when the *Spaniards* on the sea did weight
To conquer *England*, lead with vaine conceyt,   1615
    For some, our thundring *Cannons* did confound;
    Others were in the wett worlds *Empire* drownd.

1592 Vomiteting *R.*   *Final punctuation supplied at* 1595,
1610, 1616, 1617.   1608 love *R.*

Thrise did the *Queene* her high commaundment send,
I should breake vp the campe, and come away,
But after that, tenn dayes I there did spend,   1620
Makinge excuses still of my delaye,
At length I was contented to obeye,
    Weighing that in a *Soueraigne Princes* breath
    Lies th' awfull sentence both of life and death.

Now though there were great matters of suspition,   1625
Which might against me well haue beene mainteynd,
Such was my Fortunes euer blest condition,
At my retourne my wounted grace I gaind,
I was with pompe and honor enterteynd,
    My presence, gentle speach, and gestures kinde   1630
    Cleard all suspition in my Princes minde.

Like huge *Antæus*, for his strength renownd,
As dreadfull as a *Cyclops* was to sight,
When *Hercules* did cast him to the *Grownde*,
He from his Mother *Earth*, increasd his might,   1635
Euen soe when Fortune, through my foes despite,
    Gaue me the foile, when to the *Queen* I came,
    My power increasd, and I reuiud my fame.

Butt *Hatton*, then *Lord Chancellor* did dare,
To calle me *Traytor* stoutlye to my face,   1640
This man whome I advanced did not spare,
To speake great words which turnd to my disgrace,
This Man, whome I about my *Prince* did place,
    In bould attempts t' assist me at my neede,
    Did prove at length my strongest foe indeed.   1645

1624 death *R.*   1626 mainteynd *R.*   1633 *Cyclop R.*
1639 *Hatton R.*

Thus was I countercheckd by this prowd Peare,
And Him that kept fayre *Cynthias* Treasorie,
But still my favor with my soueraigne deare,
Did arme me against all adversitie,
My *Genius* or my *Dæmon* was to high,   1650
    To be supprest by my insultinge foes,
      Whose euill words did wound me, not their blowes.

Even as the *Genius* of *Marke Anthonie*
That seemd to be invincible in fight
When to *Octauius Cæsar* he drew nigh,   1655
Was euer quaild, and fearefull of his sight,
As one whose *Genius* was of greater might,
    Soe my great foes that like prowd Peckockes vanted,
      Were at my presence oft dismayd, and daunted.

Now whilst like valiant *Theseus* I did tread,   1660
The laborinth of mischiefe, and mischaunce,
My *Queene* like *Ariadne* did me lead,
Directed by a line, out of this trance,
Soe by her ayd, and royall countenaunce
    I did att last the Victorie obteyne,   1665
      And Enuie like the *Minotaure* was slaine.

Through *London* with my troopes of men I rode,
Which from the Campe at *Tilburie* I brought,
The fame of my returne, spread all abroad;
In Cittie and the suburbs round about,   1670
Men foorthwith banisht that same idle thought
    Of treazon, for the which I was suspected,
      When I as *Generall* the Campe directed.

1646 counterchecke *R.*   1649 adversite *R.*   *Punctuation*
supplied at 1652, 1662.

Thus as the Sun most broad doth shewe his face,
When he beginns in *Thetis* lappe to hide,   1675
Soe I affecting still the peoples grace,
To make my power more knowne before I died,
In pompous manner through the streets did ride,
    Casting abroad this little lastinge blaze,
    While all mens eyes did on my person gaze.   1680

Ah, how was I besotted with Ambition,
That did my brayne soe much intoxicate?
If I had wrought my gratious *Queens* perdition,
For whome both Heaven and Earth did militate,
Which way could I haue shund the Peoples hate?   1685
    If *Parmas Prince* or *Spaniards* had prevayld,
    Yet of my purpose needs I must haue faild.

For many more competitors there were,
Then left behind that would haue stept before
And ioynd their forces to put downe the *Beare*,   1690
That had begunne this mutinous vprore,
To the right *Heyre* Heauen would the crowne restore.
    Besids it happneth thus in everie state,
    Some *Treazon* loue, the most doe *Traytors* hate.

Like to *Asbestus* the *Arabian* stone,   1695
Which once made hott, cannott be cold againe,
Such is the nature of ambition,
That when it doeth possesse a prowd mans brayne,
It alwayes doth inflame his frenticke vaine,
    Which once incensd, he still doth honor craue,   1700
    Till Death approching, popps him in a grave.

Final punctuation supplied at 1680, 1681, 1692; *internal at*
1681, 1700.   1684 whome, *R.*   1690 An *R.*

The *Earle of Warwicke* in sixth *Henries* dayes,
That raisd vp kings, and after putt them downe,
To giue a kingdome, thought it greater prayse,
Than to adorne his owne head with a *Crowne;*   1705
But I deemd it a poynt of more renowne,
    To be a kinge, then others, kinges to make,
    And him vnwise, that would a *Crowne* forsake.

But sith to royall state I could not come,
I sought myselfe by office to advance,   1710
Like him that was *Dictator* made in *Rome*,
Or as the *Lord highe Constable* in *France*,
But missed of my ayme as it did chance,
    For then some mighty *Peares* my sute did crosse,
    That knew my gaine must needs haue bred their losse.   1715

I sought noe office meane, or triuialle,
But without limitation of commande,
To be the *Lord Liuetenant Generall*
Of the *Queens* forces both by sea, and land,
Whereby I might all forraine power withstand,   1720
    And if my home-borne enemies resisted,
    I might haue chopt their heads of, when I listed.

By this commission, for the which I sued,
The charge of Yorke and Wales had beene assignd,
Suffocke, and Norfocke too, it did include,   1725
My gratious *Soueraigne* was to me soe kinde,
That shee consented that it should be signd,
    But some of her Great Lords did playnely vowe
    Of this large pattent neuer to allowe.

1722 listed *R.*

[*68*]

Wise *Cicell* that first sifted mine intent,   1730
Sought vnderhand by crafte, and cunninge skill
My high-aspiring drifte to circumvent,
Yet him I labord, mutch against his will,
To rest content, my pleasure to fulfill,
But what prevayld my power against such foes,   1735
Some beinge dasht, like *Hydraes* heads more rose.

Hatton, and *Buckhurst* neuer would consent,
That to such high promotion I should rise,
But both their witts, and forces ioyntly bent
To crosse my suite, by all the subtelties,   1740
That either art, or nature could devise,
And *Hatton* would surrender the great *Seale*,
Rather than yeald to hurt the publick weale.

The Wolfe doth terrifie the gentle Lambe,
Th' *Elephant*, and *Rhinoceroth* doe fight,   1745
The Stagge dothe flye, when he dothe see a Ramme,
The Horse cannott abyde the *Camels* sight,
The beast *Hyæna* dreads the *Panthers* might,
The silly Conny, feares the wilie *Foxe*,
And kingly *Lyons* hate the crowinge *Cockes*.   1750

Soe great *Antipathie* was then betweene,
Myselfe the *Beare*, and that vnthankfull Hinde,
That hindred my great sute made to the *Queene*,
To which her priuie seale had been assignd,
For the full satisfaction of my minde;   1755
Yet men of ower degree in time of yore,
Such offices without controllment bore.

1732 drife *R.*   1736 rose *R.*   1750 *Cockes R.*

[69]

As when *Richard* the *Second* was enstald,
And crowned King, Iohn duke of *Lankaster*,
Did beare the royall sword *Cortana* cald,   1760
And as he was then *Earle of Lecester*,
The office of high *Steward* he did beare;
    As *Earle of Lincolne*, to his soueraigne Lord
    He challengd to be carver at the boord.

Thomas of Woodstocke, Duke of *Glocester*,   1765
The office of high Constable did gaine,
The *Earle of Oxford*, then cald *Robert Vere*,
Admitted was, for *Lord* high *Chamberlaine*,
The Marshalship *Lord Percye* did mainteyne,
    And Sir Iohn Dimocke, a true worthy knight,   1770
    Was the Kings Champion to defend his right.

Some of these offices vntill this hower,
By birth-right doe continue in one race,
But commonly the men of greatest power,
As they are raysed by their *Soueraignes* grace,   1775
When others fayle, or die, supply their place,
    Which one their good deserts may rest soe still
    Or els be altred at the *Princes* will.

Cromwell that *Well* which all the Abbeyes drownd,
(Come well, or ill, I will not censure it)   1780
Was made vicegerent, as a man renownd
Both for his wisedome, and his pregnant witt,
But when the Kinge in choller thought it fitt,
    He lost his place, and afterward his head,
    For some small rumours, that of him were spred.   1785

1759 King *R.*   1760 *Cortana final letter blotted R.*   1762
beare, *R.*   1765 Woodstocke *R.*   1770 Dimocke *R.*
1770–71 knigh . . . rig *R* (*frayed*).

Cardinal Woulsey, one of greater hope,
More rich, more pompous, more maiesticall,
Yorkes Great Arch-bishop, Legatt of the *Pope*,
Did beare chiefe sway by power *Pontificall*,
His pride was but the presage of his fall,   1790
    And when the King this *Prelats* death had ment,
    By dying first, he did the Kinge prevent.

Nowe of the *Duke of Somersett* I singe,
Whoe had this realmes imperiall goverment,
As *Vncle*, and *Protector* of his Kinge,   1795
He did noe hurte nor any mischiefe ment,
Yet his ambitious foes were not content,
    To take his head without sufficient cause,
    But halfe his lande, contrarie to the Lawes.

Would I could soe haue tempred my highe thought   1800
Or with soe milde a grace had been endued;
But if my wish had to effect been brought,
Perhaps the Prince and Commons might haue rued,
And such *Catastrophees* might haue ensued,
    That England should not without stormes of teares,   1805
    Beholde the purple gore of slaughtred *Peares*.

Like *Tantalus*, I saw th' Hesperian fruict,
Which when I would haue tasted, fled awaye,
The Heauens compeld me to surcease my suite,
When I beyonde my limits sought to swaye,   1810
Vnconstant Fortune offerd me foule play,
    But passion ruld me, and my *Soueraignes* favor
    Made me presume, on *Fortune* that did waver.

1790 pride, *R.*   1797 content,, *R.*   1802 brought *R.*

O then lett not the *Soueraigne Monarch* trust,
To anie one peculier Potentate,   1815
That ruleth not by reason, but by lust,
Soe consequently brings himselfe in hate,
And doth endanger his dread *Princes* state:
    This makes me wishe, none such, I beeinge dead,
    May of the *Prince*, like me, be favored.   1820

Edward the Seconds love to *Gavestone*,
Stird vp through all the Realme great murmuringe,
Richard the *Seconds* mighty favor showne
To *Robert Vere*, did greeuos trouble bringe,
Queene Margarett, by too much favoringe   1825
    Proud *De la Poole*, wrought good Duke Humphreyes fall
    And lost at length her husband, crowne, and all.

But lett me aske, what hath my Soueraigne lost,
By favoringe myselfe, or my greate blood?
It may be that through Envie I was croste,   1830
Not that I did oppugne my Countries good,
Perhaps my foes in policie withstoode
    My highe attempts, doubtinge if I aspird
    Like *Clymenes* sonne, their howses might be fyerd.

The *Duke of Venice*, as th' Italians saye,   1835
Is counted but an honorable *Slaue*.
He beares the Name, his Senators beare sway,
And hath a double voice, nor more can crave,
But as in Oxford heads of howses haue.
    Were I a Duke, (as I was little lesse,)   1840
    Such Demy-Peares should not my powre suppresse.

Final punctuation supplied at 1834, 1836, 1839, 1841.   1836
honrable *R.*   1841 Deny- *R.*

Aye me, that euer honor should be checkt,
By men to vs inferior in degree,
But why should we that were great Lords, expect,
Enthrald to sinne, from mallice to be free?   1845
From th' eye of Heauen O whither can we flee?
    Death as a Catch-pole comes, when wee think lest,
    And doth for debt to Nature, vs arrest.

I little did regard what *Solon* sayd,
Respect the end, consider what thou art,   1850
Noe man is blest till he in grave be layd,
And after Death hath strooke him with his dart,
His Soule doth to celestiall bliss depart;
    "For this is certeyne that the end doth shewe
    "Whether a man be happie, yea, or noe.   1855

When from the Court, a Malecontent I went,
Crost in my suite, late hoping to be blest,
Death shortly did my purposes prevent,
Giuing Ambitious thoughts eternall rest,
That erst soe hottly boyled in my brest,   1860
    Yet Life was sweete, and I was loth to leaue it,
    But death was sower, yet forc'd I did receaue it.

A little while before death did approache,
For certaine truth, as divers men doe say,
Piggs followed me as I road in my coach,   1865
Which by noe meanes could then be driuen awaye,
It is most true, while I on earth did staye,
    Many vnthankfull Piggs by me did thriue,
    Which now of prayse my worthy deeds depriue.

Internal commas supplied at 1842, 1845, 1864.   1844 By *R.*
1859 thoughth *R.*   1862 it *R.*

If Piggs did haunt me as Familier Sprites,   1870
It is not strainge they shewed my death drew neare.
To *Brutus* and to *Dion*, some few nights
Before their deathes *Hobgoblines* did appeare,
I speake not this my guiltie life to cleare,
    But that the simpler sort of men may knowe   1875
    Such sightes, like Comets, Princes Deaths forshewe.

I kept a Spirite in a Chrystall boxe
Which of a Bridge, or Bathe bad me beware,
But Oh the Fiend, more subtle than a Foxe,
Doth giue such Oracles as doubtfull are,   1880
Thereby to catch men sooner in his snare,
    Yet in some sort his woord did fall out true,
    As you shall finde, by that which doth ensue.

Deepe learned Socrates, that hath been deemd,
By *Phœbus Oracle* the wisest wight,   1885
Whoe was of Gods, and men highly esteemd,
For wisdoms loue, that Ages only light,
Had often with him a Familiar Sprite,
    That hindred him from serving sensuall lust,
    To doe things that are lawfull, good, and iust.   1890

Oh had I had a Spirite of that kinde,
To mooue me to good deeds, I had bin blest,
Then hade I borne a more submissiue minde,
But that ill Sprite Ambition soe possesst
The inward motions of my sinfull breast,   1895
    That it provockt me still to doe amisse,
    And erre from the right way that leads to blisse.

1870 Sprits, *R.*   *Final punctuation supplied at* 1871, 1880,
1897.   1872 nights, *R.*   1876 *Blot at end R.*   1883 A *R.*
1896 deoe *R.*

[74]

When I from *Rycott* towards Bathe did ride,
Some that did make fayre shewes prou'd to vnkinde.
I tooke a dramme to much, whereof I died,   1900
Much sicke in body, but more sicke in minde,
When I my trusted servaunts, false did finde,
     But what could pompe, or worldly wealth availe?
     Even they betrayd my life that cride all hayle.

Henrie the Fowrth by wizards was foretould,   1905
His lott was in *Hierusalem* to dye,
His voyage he determined to hold
Towards the *Holie Lande*, his chance to trye,
But whilest the King at *Westminster* did lie,
     He fell soare sicke, and dyed heare in this Ream   1910
     In th' Abbots Chamber cald *Hierusalem*.

Kinge *Pyrrhus* end was thus prognosticate,
That when he sawe a Bull, and woolfe to fight,
Deaths strocke should cancell his lifes vtmost date,
In *Argos* he beheld that fatall sight   1915
Of these two beasts, in Copper carved right,
     Seeming to fight, and there as he did ride,
     Was with a *Tile-stone* hurt, and shortly died.

Nowe I forgott, what my *Familiar* sayd,
That of a Bath did warne me to take heede,   1920
Or els by me it was not rightly wayed:
The name of *Bath* was ominous indeede,
For riding toward Bathe, my Bane did breede,
     Thus Destinies are oftentimes foreshowne,
     But not auoyded, though they maye be knowne.   1925

Final punctuation supplied at 1899, 1903 (*R frayed*), 1918, 1921,
1925.   1907 detrmined *R.*   1910 dyd *R, possibly* Realm
R.   1914 Death *R.*   1915 fatetall *R.*   1919 Nnowe *R.*
1925 thy *R.*

I meant t' haue left my wief at *Killingwoorth*,
Where She perhaps might during life haue stayd,
Whilst vnder an ill Plannett I road foorth,
Some secret to one man I open sayd,
Which after to my ruine was bewrayde.   1930
   As some by chainge of loues may be defield,
   Soe some by change of cupps haue beene beguild.

As *Alexander* in a goulden cupp
Distaind with poyson dranke his deadly drought
When hee in stately *Babilon* did supp,   1935
His death (that woone all battayles which he fought)
By *Antipaters* treacherie was wrought,
   And now his bodie in small compass lies,
   Whome one worlds Conquest once could scarse suffice.

Soe I dranke Poyson, and forgott straightway   1940
That I was *Earle of Lester* any more,
But a small lumpe of Earth, and clod of claye,
Whom the still-wavering world admird of yore
And few or none, now being dead, deplore,
   But like a shaddow, from reflecting glasse,   1945
   As from their eyes soe out of mind I passe.

Thus I that oftentimes did lie in waight
T' entrappe the liues of others in a snare,
Was catcht myself, entangled with the bayte
Which wretched I, for others did prepare;   1950
Of inward foes, men hardly can beware:
   Great *Agamemnons* death whoe doth not rue?
   Whom *Troians* feard, him lewd *Ægystus* slue.

Final punctuation supplied at 1927, 1930, 1931, 1936, 1938,
1942, 1945, 1946; *internal at* 1944.   1949 bayte, *R.*   1951
foes men, *R.*   1952 *Agamennons R.*

Loe heare the period of lifes last date,
Euen in the height of my prosperitie,   1955
Cutt of from life by some vntimely Fate,
The *Beare* sprunge from Northumberland did dye,
When he presumed to haue climbd most highe:
   Whom being yet aliue noe man could tame,
   Nowe beeinge dead, ten thousand men doe blame.   1960

I merveyle why some people doe suppose,
That I for feare least I should be accusde,
Poysned myselfe, as vrgd by mighty foes,
That I my prince and country had abusde,
I knew my faults might either be excusde,   1965
   Or that the *Queene* my follies might forgiue,
   For neuer did a Prince more gratious liue.

How could I putt so little confidence
In my deere Soveraygns long-approved grace?
Had I not many tymes experience   1970
Of her firme favor in a doubtful case?
When fortune turnd from mee her smiling face?
   What cause had I to fall into dispayre?
   That might beg pardon at her mercye chayre.

Say that I should bee iudged by the law,   1975
Her will might lawes severitye restrayne,
The beare but of the Lyon stood in awe,
Of her alone mercy I might obteyne:
And Anacharsis speetch was tru and playne
   That laws like spiders webbs hold fast smale flys,   1980
   But Drones escape, and breake the net that tyes.

1966 forgiue *R.*   1969 grace, *R.*   1980 flys *R.*

Graue *Cato* did himselfe vnwisely slay,
Because he would not yeald to *Cæsars* will,
Scorning his Countries Tirant to obeye,
I doubt not but the fact was very ill,   1985
In any heathen, that himselfe did kill,
    But in a *Christian*, I account it worse
    That to his sinne will add soe great a curse.

Now sith this sinne is odious in gods sight,
And he that slayes himselfe, accursed dies,   1990
Sith in the world I wanted noe delight,
And liud at Court, as in th' earths Paradise,
Censure me not soe wicked or vnwise,
    To seeke my owne death, to prevent my fall,
    Although my crymes had beene most capitall.   1995

O thou poore *Travayler* that passest bye
The place of my past glories monument
In *Warwicke Towne*, where my dead corps doth lye
Poorely interd by frends too negligent,
Sith Potentates voutchsafe not to lament,   2000
    I pray the, honest frend, if heare thou come,
    Graue ruth vppon thy brest, prayse on my toomb.

Thou mightst haue seene some of the noble peares
With humble congeys do me reverence.
I tell thee, Man, there haue not many yeares   2005
Slided away by tract of time, sith-thence
Meane men haue quaket at my magnificence,
    I was envide, beloud, or feard of alle,
    And when I frowned, halfe the Court lookt pale.

1995 cryms *R.*   *Final punctuation supplied at* 1999, 2004,
2008.   2001 the *R.*   2005 thee *R.*

Pompey the great that long did seigniorize,   2010
Amonge the *Conscript* Fathers of old *Rome*,
And whylom many lands did Monarchize,
Yet when by *Cæsar* he was ouercome,
He being dead did want a worthy tombe,
   Thus *Pompey* liud, thus did great *Pompey* dy;   2015
   Thus *Lester* liud, thus doth Great *Lester* lye.

Soe one my graue a Marble stone is layd,
Bare stone, weake Loue, soone hott and quickly cold,
My Corps that sometyme was soe richly rayd
In *Tyrian* purple, pearle, and cloth of gold,   2020
Nowe shrowded vnder a base earthly mold,
   Showes vnto them, which haue my person seene,
   But the bare shadowe, of what I haue beene.

Thou mightst haue seene engraven on my browe,
Characters of Nobilitie and grace,   2025
And noted me, whose knee did neuer bow,
But if great *Ioue* or *Cynthia* were in place,
My port, my pompe, my presence, and my pace,
   Shewed that I was a man to greatnes borne,
   Whose thoughts all base seruillitie did scorne.   2030

Thou mightst haue seen a stately personage,
And framd to that a corespondent mind,
The rarest Politician of that Age,
Whose disposition it was hard to find,
Prudent in peace, not mutch to warre enclind,   2035
   Nor Ruld soe mutch by reason as by passion,
   I was a man conformd to each Mans fashion.

2015 dy *R.*   2020 cloth, *R.*   2026 me *R.*   2029 borne
R.   2030 surrillitie *R* (*? for* scurrillitie); scorne, *R.*

Courteous with *Cæsar*, sterne with *Tamberlaine*,
Gratious with *Scipio*, graue with *Pericles*,
Seuere with *Cato*, bould with *Charlemaine*,   2040
Factious with *Sylla*, mild with *Socrates*,
Portly with *Pompey*, proud with *Damocles*,
   Observing minds, myself I wisely carried,
   And fitting all mens minds, from all I varried.

Pilgrimme, farewell, but ere thou part from hence,   2045
At euerie word let fall a brackish teare,
Write this small *Epitaphe* in my defence,
Heare Lester lies, old Englands peareless Peare,
Whome those that did not love were forst to feare:
   Farewell once more, and say that I am gonne,   2050
   But to discover regions, yet vnknowne.

Now since I walked in the path of Death,
My frinds, my kinne, my poets me forsooke.
Noe learned muse bestowed her gentle breath,
In breathing forth my prayse, nor vndertooke   2055
To register my honors in her booke,
   And of my fame noe monuments are left
   In gratitude, and Tyme hath all bereft.

Thrise happie were those valiant Lords of *Rome*,
Whose statues, brought into the *Capitoll*,   2060
Were there erected by the *Senats* doome,
But cheefely when the Muses did inroule
Their names in honors everlasting scrowle,
   Who when their conquering corps to death did yeald
   Were solemly interd in *Mars-is field*.   2065

Internal commas supplied at 2042, 2044; *final punctuation at*
2048, 2053, 2057, 2060, 2065.   2060 statutes *R*.

But whoe erects an Image to my fame?
Who consecrats Colosses to my prayse?
Who studies to immortalize my name?
Who doth a stately *Pyramid* vprayse
T' entoombe my corps, that slept in *Cynthias* dayes?   2070
  Who sunge the Requiem or in mornfull verse
  Fixt my due prayse vppon my sable hearse.

Ere I could come neare to th' *Elysian Camps*,
Hauing a tedious pilgrimage to make
There, where Cœlestiall Earth-illightning Lamps   2075
Did neuer shine, I did my way mistake,
And soe fell downe in *Lethes* sleepy lake,
  Loe thus my Name, through *Europe* once renowned,
  Now in Oblivions muddy pitt is drowned.

Bucephalus Great *Alexanders Horse*   2080
That did his kinge good service in the Field,
Was soe esteemd that over his dead corse
A goodlie citty this dread Prince did build;
Noe towne, nor worthy tombe doth my corps shield
  From Fortunes malice: is it not great pitty?   2085
  Lords want fayre toombes, while beasts ly in the cittie.

My brother *Ambross*, and myselfe did climbe,
As high as subiects fortunes could permitt,
Wee once were great and florisht in the prime,
Myghty in power, and prompt inough of witt,   2090
But since that wee were falne into Deaths pitt
  Owre flesh scarce witherd, and our bones scarce rotten,
  Owre fame is dead and wee are quite forgotten.

Final punctuation supplied at 2070, 2078, 2092.   2071 Wo *R.*
2072 pray *R.*

Thus our well pampred flesh is turnd to dust.
We haue beene *Troians*, *Ilium* sometyme stoode,   2095
The Heauens in cancelling our days were iust.
We fed on Ioyes, but now for wormes are foode
Who while we liued, for our countries good,
   Bore vp the Ragged Staffe, which oft was seene
   Aduanc'd in honor of our gratious *Queene*.   2100

Nowe the short Springtyme of our pompe is past,
The tedious Autumne of our fall is come.
What thinge beneath the moone can ever last.
The Foxe, the Asse, the Ape possest our roome
And triumpht in our dreadfull dayes of doome,   2105
   Yea nowe the Ragged Staffe once borne so high
   Is broken and in dust the beares doe lie.

And *Cynthia* whome my Spirit doth adore,
Vp to her *Spheare* Cœlestiall having fled,
Will with her presence grace this soyle no more   2110
Sith her best frends are now prest downe or dead.
O Powers Immortall, decke her royall head
   With an eternall *Crowne*, and let her rest,
   Amonge the Sacred Queens, and Virgins blest.

When Death, as true iacke of the clocke doth strike   2115
And Fortune turnes the wheele of chance about,
Crœsus, and *Irus*, then are both alike,
The Ritch and poore, the feeble and the stoute,
Mans life euen like a *Taper* burneth out;
   And when the Howerglasse of his tyme is runne,   2120
   Atropoes cutts the threede, which *Clotho* spunne.

All punctuation supplied at 2094, 2096, 2098, 2101, 2102, 2108,
2109, 2111.   2101 Springgtyme *R;* ouer *R.*   2118 poore *R.*

What resteth nowe for me, but to lament
My sinns that are to many to be told.
I do confesse my trespas, and repent,
In doing good, I was too slacke and could,   2125
In doing ill, I was to quicke and bould,
    For mercye now I call, I plead, I crie,
    For want of grace, I sigh, I faint, I die.

If any grace to me my greife could winne,
Would I had heare an *Ocean* fraught with teares   2130
To ouerflowe the mountayne of my sinne,
O would could sighs could pierce the flinty *Spheres*
And moue to pittie, the Cœlestiall eares.
    Would I had ayre to sigh, or seas to weepe,
    Or would my soule were with my corps asleepe.   2135

Yet though my sinns passe number as the sands,
O mortall men, to Him the iudgment leave
That dwells in Temples neuer built with hands.
Your Iudgment may perhaps yourselues deceive.
Noe torment shall my Soule of hope bereave.   2140
    Some thinke some diuells haue an hope of grace;
    Keepe you your *Faith* and I will *Hope* imbrace.

O Yearth and Ashes, wherefore dost thou boast
Of pompe, of honor, or of riches store;
All this I gaind, this gaine I quite haue lost.   2145
I gaind but losse when death knockt at my dorr.
Poore *Iob* himselfe was neuer halfe so poore,
    For I lay naked when to earth I fell in:
    Heauen couers him that hath noe howse to dwell in.

2122 lament, *R.*   *Final punctuation supplied at* 2123, 2128,
2133, 2135, 2136, 2138, 2139, 2140, 2141, 2145, 2146, 2147,
2148; *internal at* 2137, 2143.   2132 sighs *Emend.*] *Om. R.*
2142 you Faith *R.*   2146 knock *R.*

Farewell ye Lords, that in fayre *Albion* swaye,   2150
Cutt not the *Gordian* knott of loue in twayne.
With Loyall harts your *Souueraigns* will obey.
Iustice and right with all your strength mainteyne
That Heauen one you may peace and plentie raine.
   What was amisse in me doe you amend.   2155
   If ought were good, that follow to your end.

If of yourselues good goverment ye lacke,
Ye are vnfitt the publique weale to guide,
Your vassals, and your slaues behinde your backe,
Will laughe to scorne the follie of your pride.   2160
A conscience cleane, all sclanders may deride:
   Vse vertue as an Antidote most stronge,
   Against the poyson of a venomd tongue.

Adieu, fayre Dames that grace this Earthly globe
Where in her golden *Hemicycle* sate   2165
The *Nights* pale *Queene*, yclad in royal Robe,
Exempt from earth, by him that ruleth Fate,
Preserue the reputation of your state:
   Honor the Kinge, that doth like Phœbus shine,
   Whome ye may tearme humane, and halfe diuine.   2170

Farewell, ye Learned Iudges of this land,
Iudge ye vprightly least yee iudged bee
When ye before great *Radamanth* shall stand.
If once condemnd, ye neuer can be free.
It is enacted thus by *Heauens* decree: 2175
   The gods will call a *Parlament* on high
   To which ye shall be summond when ye dye.

Final punctuation supplied at 2150–52, 2156, 2160, 2166–67,
2169–71, 2174–75, 2177; *internal at* 2164, 2171, 2174.   2157
y lacke, R.

Farewell my Sonne, *Robert* my sonne farewell.
Proceede in vertue as thou hast begunne;
So maiest thou thy progenitors excell.   2180
Likely thou art a better race to runne,
Make thy dead sire blest in his livinge sonne;
 Sith all my hope in thee doth only rest,
 Fixe vertue and true honor in thy brest.

O *Heauens*, rayne showers of glorie one the throne   2185
Of Ieames the King that now in peace doth raigne,
Who doth possess the *Patriarch Iacobs* Stone
Which doth to him of aintient right perteyne.
Euen all the dayes of heaven lett him remayne
 An happy Kinge to rule this happy soyle,   2190
 To trivmph still and giue his foes the foyle.

So shalle the Warlicke Brittaines fame encrease
And to the height of happines aspire,
Euen till the *Spheares* swift mouement shal cease,
When Heauen shale melt, and *Earth* consume with fyre, 2195
Adieu, vaine world; my Ghoast must now retyre,
 To vnfrequented dezarts, ther to staye,
 Till all flesh turne to dust and slimie claye.

Final punctuation supplied at 2178–80, 2182–83, 2186, 2188,
2190. 2185 *Heauens R;* thron *R (frayed).* 2196 Adieu *R.*

[*85*]

The Authors Conclusion.

Let noe man thinke, I exorcizd the Ghoast
Of this great Peare, that sleepeth in the dust,
Or coniurd vp his Spirit to this coast,
To presse him with disprayse, or prayse uniust.
I am not partiall, but giue him his due,   5
And to his sowle I wish eternall health,
Ne doe I thinke all written tales are true,
That are incerted in his Commonwealth.
What others wrote before, I doe reuiue,
But am not like to them, incensd with hate,   10
And as I playnely write, soe doe I striue
To write the truth, not wronginge his estate:
   Of whom it may be sayd, and censurd well,
   He both in vice, and vertue, did excell.

All italic in R; heading R only.   1 exorcizd *RT]* exercis'd
PXAB.   14 *B appends:* Iamque opus exegi, / Deus dedit
his quoque finem.; *AB add:* FINIS.

Notes

These minimal notes are restricted to problems in the text. They do not sketch the historical background nor probe the validity of the *Commonwealth* libels. They ignore classical allusions, medieval references, and Renaissance literary commonplaces. For identification of Leicester's friends and enemies, see the Index.

The relation of the *Ghost* to its primary source may be summarized in a concordance of passages citing, for each relevant stanza, the page on which the topic *begins* in the 1584 *Copie of a Leter:*

St. 23	P. 15	St. 96	P. 31	St. 134	P. 111
30	80	98	32	136	103
32	80, 29	100	33	139	167
34	51, 63	102	34	143	190
36	66	104	44	144	53
37	89	106	34, 44	153	100
39	46	108	56	154	105
40	60	110	56	157	120
50	52, 46	112	56	160	121
69	37	116	163	162–68	128
72	39	123	67	170	118
78	20	124	73	172	106
87	27	125	73, 69	175	95, 112
90	25	126	72	227	19
92	28, 35	127	77	260	178
94	28	133	71	266	20

Title motto. Juvenal, *Satires* IX. 118 ff. The conventional Latin distich to Zoilus (p. 5) appears to be original.

Lines 8–10. Cf. Rogers, *Celestiall Elegies*, sig. A8.

29–32. A clear verbal echo of Spenser, *Ruines of Rome*, sonnet 14.

36–42. The stanza is patterned on the opening of "The Ballade of a Bee," a popular political piece on Essex: "It was a time when seely Bees coulde speake / And in that time, I was a seely Bee." Rogers cannot use the original pun on time/thyme. One of the numerous manuscripts of this poem is interestingly found in the volume containing *Ghost* MS. *T.*

119. *necks*. To clarify the pun, see *NED* neck sb.² Obs.

190–95. Adapted from Spenser, *Ruines of Time*, ll. 365–71 (one line verbatim).

211n. Apparently Agrippa 1. 2.

218. *Iulio*. Indexed as Borgarucci.

Notes

253. *Barkly.* Late hand in MS. *T* comments: "The Lord Berkley after his [Leicester's] death recovered it againe." The facts are extraliterary.

291–92. *men.* Identified by *Commonwealth* as Layton and Paulet (see Index).

322. Ignorance of the poet's source leaves the sense uncertain (note variants).

348–51. *Chronicles.* The poet's direct source seems to have been Drayton, *Mortimeriados,* lines 2157–59 (supplying rhyme at 344–46).

375. *shake.* The rejected reading is possible (see *NED* strake v.⁴).

512n. Or rather, I *alias* 3 Kings 4:30; Josephus, *Antiquities* 8. 2. 5.

534. *Lachryma Christi.* The scribes (*R* missing) were unable to cope with this standard item of the hedonistic menu (cf. Marlowe, 2 *Tamburlaine* 1. 6. 96).

544. *Barwicke.* All *Ghost* texts show this error for *Warwick* (as established at p. 20 of 1584 *Copie* and the great majority of extant manuscripts, including the seven at the Folger Library). However, a sampling of twelve of the British Museum manuscripts of the *Commonwealth* shows *one* with the *Barwicke* reading (MS. Lansdowne 215, fol. 13), the error resulting from the strange resemblance of one form of fancy secretary *W* to *B*. In brief, this textual error establishes the presumption that Rogers did not work with a printed copy but with a manuscript of this nature. Then as now, *Commonwealth* manuscripts were commoner than the suppressed printed text.

606. *Abbingdon.* This authentic detail exemplifies facts derived from sources other than the *Commonwealth.* In this instance it may have been oral tradition at the poet's Gloucester Hall, where Amy Robsart's corpse rested before the funeral in St. Mary's.

617n. Virgil, *Aeneid* 3. 56–57 (cf. 4. 412).

632. The young poet was obviously ignorant of the cardinal's apostasy.

647. *naturall.* Namely, two natural children. The survivor was Robert of line 2178.

655. *ingled.* The preferred reading is supported by common linkage of *ingle* with *underhand,* as in Thomas Middleton, *The Roaring Girl* 4. 2. (Mermaid, 2. 78).

682. *Throgmorton.* No animosity toward Leicester (nor hint of poison) appears in the anonymous "tragedy," *The Legend of Sir Nicholas Throckmorton,* ed. J. G. Nichols (Roxburghe Club, 1874).

725. *Killigray.* Curiously, Killigrew started out as Throckmorton's waiting man. He was still a groom of the Privy Chamber after 1600.

748. *Ape.* An allusion to Elizabeth's nickname for Simier, *singe* o monkey. Alençon was her "frog." Observe the monkey in the French 158 woodcut.

Notes

778. *Gates.* Rogers has embroidered the incident with details adapted from *The Spanish Tragedy;* see F. T. Bowers, "Kyd's Pedringano: Sources and Parallels," *Harvard Studies and Notes* 13 (1931): 241–49.

860n. Juvenal, *Satires* 14. 204–5.

903. *liues.* Alluding to the execution of Somerset's brother Thomas.

904. Apparently invented by Rogers, the archery story was incorporated into Peter Heylyn's *Ecclesia Restaurata* (1661), p. 150, whence it is cited as sober history by a modern biographer of Edward VI.

953. *familiar.* The "familiars" at 953 and 1877 are the poet's invention, imitating the well-known Jerusalem anecdote at 1905.

995. MS. *T* has marginal note in late hand, "Dudley and Empson."

1077. As *Commonwealth* verifies (p. 105), Arbella's triumvirate were the grandmother, Bess of Hardwick, Countess of Shrewsbury; uncle, Gilbert, later earl; and proposed father-in-law, Leicester. The death of Lord Denbigh 19 July 1584 occurred too late for notice in the *Commonwealth*.

1093. The boring review of the succession in stanzas 157–168 (deleted from the abridged *Ghost*) can be checked from other accounts. Misled by the obscurity of the *Commonwealth*, Rogers has omitted one generation at 1147–48.

1199. *Queene.* Mary of Scotland; *she* (1201) is Elizabeth.

1205. The animal heraldry, chiefly from official crests, is clear: Bear, Dudley; Red Lion, Scotland (Stuarts); Bull, Hastings (Huntingdon); Wolf, unsolved; Phoenix, Seymour. The Eagle, allegorical rather than heraldic, apparently represents James.

1295. Elizabeth's fury over this title is ignored by the poet.

1317n. *Sir.* Yorke was *not* a knight; Stanley was.

1349n. *Plinie. Natural History* 10. 69 (flamingo).

1352. *daughters.* The *RX* reading is confirmed by Stow's account of Leicester's banquet 23 July 1586, with "countie Egmounts daughters" among the guests (*STC* 23334, p. 1245). Presumably the copyist construed *P* 1352n as "daughter's."

1394n. *Satires* 7. 199–200. Rogers or his source misunderstood the reference to [King Servius] Tullius as applying to Cicero (1396 ff.).

1494. Stanzas 214–216 echo passages in bk. I of Castiglione's *Il Cortegiano* (Raleigh's 1900 edition of the Hoby translation, pp. 91, 96, 97, 88, 118, 85). Hoby's widow figures in the poet's biography.

1550. *suffice.* Required by rhyme, the emendation is supported by 1939.

1647. Burghley (cf. 1730).

1752. *Hinde.* Hatton's crest. Compare the beast heraldry at 1205.

1758ff. The poet's legal antiquities are mostly irrelevant.

Notes

1863. The curious pig story is otherwise unknown.

1898. *Bathe.* Factual error does not spoil the fiction. Leicester was on his annual journey to the baths at Buxton.

1926. The reference to Lettice hints awareness of the rumor that she managed the poisoning (see Introduction, MS. *X*). *Killingwoorth* was the usual Elizabethan form for *Kenilworth.*

1999. The earl's elaborate lament over his shabby interment shows that the poem predates the uncertain year when Lettice built the imposing monument at Warwick. This was after 1602, it is clear from a letter by William Poyntz, Leicester's servant for seventeen years (*Calendar of Hatfield MSS* 12. 403).

Index of Persons in Leicester's Ghost

Supplementing the notes, this index identifies people of the period 1530–1610 who are named or referred to in the text. Most are in *DNB*. Date of death is given if known, and the citations are by line number.

Allen, Thomas, Oxford scholar (1632), 204
Arbella Stuart, Princess (1615), 1071, 1199
Berkeley, Henry, seventh Baron Berkeley (1613), 253
Borgarucci, Julio, royal physician (1581?), 218
Butler, Thomas, tenth earl of Ormonde (1614), 723
Carey, George, second Baron Hunsdon (1603), 296
Carey, Henry, first Baron Hunsdon (1596), 289
Cecil, William, first Baron Burghley (1598), 1647, 1730
Coligni, Odet de, cardinal of Chatillon (1571), 624
Cromwell, Thomas, earl of Essex (1540), 1779
Dee, John, astrologer (1608), 204
Devereux, Robert, second earl of Essex (executed 1601), 673
Devereux, Robert, third earl of Essex (1646), 678
Devereux, Walter, first earl of Essex (1576), 652
Doughty, Thomas (executed 1578), 764
Drake, Sir Francis, admiral (1596), 767
Dudley, Ambrose, earl of Warwick, Leicester's brother (1590), 281, 2087ff
Dudley *née* Robsart, Amy, Leicester's wife (1560), 603, 638
Dudley, Edmund, statesman, Leicester's grandfather (executed 1510), 995
Dudley, Guilford, husband of next, Leicester's brother (executed 1554), 937
Dudley *née* Grey, Jane, "queen" (executed 1554), 50, 935ff.
Dudley, John, duke of Northumberland, Leicester's father (executed 1553), 43, 695, 890, 1957
Dudley *née* Knollys, Lettice, widow of Essex, Leicester's wife (1634), 288, 660, 744, 1926
Dudley, Robert, earl of Leicester (1588), passim
Dudley, Robert, "duke of Northumberland," Leicester's son by Sheffield (1649), 642, 2178
Dudley, Robert, "Lord Denbigh," Leicester's son by Lettice (1584), 1070
Edward VI, King (1553), 891, 904, 927ff, 958, 1795
Egmont, Lamoral, count of Egmont (1568), 1352
Elizabeth I, Queen (1603), passim
Farnese, Alexander, duke of Parma (1593), 1686
Fitzalan, Henry, twelfth earl of Arundel (1580), 929
Fleetwood, William, recorder of London (1594), 299

Index of Persons

Gates, ———, Leicester's servant (hanged 1583), 778

Grey, Arthur, fourteenth Baron Grey de Wilton (1593), 290

Grey, Henry, duke of Suffolk (executed 1554), 935, 952

Hastings *née* Dudley, Catherine, countess, Leicester's sister (1620), 282

Hastings, Henry, third earl of Huntingdon, Leicester's brother-in-law (1595), 282, 1086, 1198, 1207

Hatton, Sir Christopher, lord chancellor (1591), 1639, 1737

Henry VIII, King (1547), 941, 956, 1783

Henry III of France, previously duc d'Anjou (1589), 629

Herbert, Henry, second earl of Pembroke, m. Leicester's niece (1601), 286

Hopton, Sir Owen, lieutenant of the Tower (ca. 1597), 293

Horsey, Sir Edward, soldier (1583), 295

Howard, Thomas, fourth duke of Norfolk (exec. 1572), 806, 917

Hunnis, Robert (Robin), son of poet William, page to Essex, 668

Isabella of Austria, Infanta of Spain (1633), 1099

James I, King (1625), dedication, 13, 579, 1198, 1210, 1268, 2169, 2186

Killigrew (Killigray), William, retainer, later of Privy Chamber, 725

Leighton (Layton), Sir Thomas, captain of Guernsey, kin to Lettice (1611?), 291

Lopez (Lopus), Roderigo, royal physician (executed 1594), 218

Mary I, Queen (1558), 43n, 48, 51, 71, 936ff, 998

Mary Stuart, queen of Scotland (executed 1587), 814, 1068

Norris, Sir John, soldier (1597), 1317

Paulet, Sir Amias, lieutenant governor of Jersey (1588), 291

Radcliffe, Thomas, third earl of Sussex (1583), 555, 694

Russell, Francis, second earl of Bedford, father-in-law of Leicester's brother (1585), 283

Sackville, Thomas, first earl of Dorset (1608), 1737

Salvadore, Italian ruffian in Leicester's service, 750

Seymour, Edward, duke of Somerset (executed 1552), 894, 907, 925, 1793

Seymour, Edward, first earl of Hertford (1621), 1208

Seymour, Thomas, Baron Seymour (executed 1549), 903

Sheffield *née* Howard, Douglas, Lady Sheffield, Leicester's mistress (1608), 641

Sheffield, John, second Baron Sheffield (1568), 643

Sidney, Sir Henry, lord deputy of Ireland, Leicester's brother-in-law (1586), 285

Sidney, Sir Philip, soldier, Leicester's nephew (1586), 1326

Simier, Jean de, French courtier, 736

Stanley, Sir William, adventurer (1630), 1322

Stewart *née* Douglas, Margaret, countess of Lennox (1578), 709

Talbot *née* Hardwick, Elizabeth, countess of Shrewsbury (1608), 1077

Talbot, Gilbert, seventh earl of Shrewsbury, stepson of preceding (1616), 1077

Throckmorton (Frogmorton), Sir Nicholas, diplomat (1571), 682

Valois, Francis, duc d'Alençon (1584), 541

Wolsey, Thomas, Cardinal (1530), 1786

Wriothesley, Thomas, first earl of Southampton (1550), 929

Yorke, Rowland, soldier (1588), 1319

The Renaissance English Text Society was founded to publish scarce literary texts, chiefly nondramatic, of the period 1475–1660. Normally during each subscription year two single volumes, or one double volume, will be distributed to members, who may also purchase previous publications of the society, while supplies last, at membership rates. The subscription rate is ten dollars per series, payable in advance; bills for renewals are issued on completion of each series. Subscriptions should be sent to the secretary-treasurer, James M. Wells, at the Newberry Library, 60 West Walton Street, Chicago, Illinois 60610. Institutional members are requested to provide, at the time of enrollment, any order numbers or other information required for their billing records; the society cannot provide multiple invoices or other complex forms for their needs. Nonmembers may buy copies of the first publication, at a higher rate than to members, from Mr. Wells, and of subsequent volumes from the University of Chicago Press, 11030 South Langley Avenue, Chicago, Illinois 60628.

First Series

Vol. I. *Merie Tales of the Mad Men of Gotam*, by A. B., edited by Stanley J. Kahrl, and *The History of Tom Thumbe*, by R. I., edited by Curt F. Bühler, 1965.

Vol. II. Thomas Watson's Latin *Amyntas*, edited by Walter F. Staton, Jr., and Abraham Fraunce's translation, *The Lamentations of Amyntas*, edited by Franklin M. Dickey, 1967.

Second Series

Vol. III. *The dyaloge called Funus*, a translation of Erasmus's colloquy (1534), & *A very pleasaunt & fruitful Diologe called The Epicure*, Gerrard's translation of Erasmus's colloquy (1545), edited by Robert R. Allen, 1969.

Vol. IV. *Leicester's Ghost*, by Thomas Rogers, edited by Franklin B. Williams, Jr., 1972.

Third Series

Vol. V–VI. *A Collection of Emblems*, by George Wither, with introduction by Rosemary Freeman and bibliographical notes by Charles J. Hensley, *in press*.